Acclaim for Steven Pres

Steve has ripped the band-aid off. The wounds underneath are the scars created on the path to mastery. I was actually crying in the middle. Steve shows in this book what that pain looks like."

James Altucher - Author, Entrepreneur

"Steven Pressfield is a writing hero. I loved the chance to see this master of story tell his own story."

Jeff Glor, CBS News

"**Govt Cheese** is exactly what I need right now: A true story of overcoming obstacles, both internal and external, to lead a life the author could barely dream of when he was starting out. I recommend this book to anyone who wishes they could finally take their shot at living the life of they secretly know they deserve."

Brian Koppelman - writer/co-creator of "Billions" and "Rounders"

In the Evolution genre the protagonist's unrealized potential evolves over time until it reaches its full humanity. Steven Pressfield's amazing memoir arcs this most demanding form with insight, power and beauty."

Robert McKee - Author/ Lecturer

"Steven Pressfield's **Govt Cheese** is a **Down and Out in Paris and London** for our time. A memoir told with equal parts humility, humor and heartbreak, Pressfield takes the reader on his twenty-seven-year odyssey, imparting the most elusive of traits, not just for the artist or writer but for us all—wisdom."

Jack Carr - #1 NYT bestselling author of the James Reece "Terminal List" series.

GOVT CHEESE

a memoir

Also by Steven Pressfield

STEVEN
PRESSFIELD

GOVT CHEESE

a memoir

Sarsaparilla Media LLC
Los Angeles, CA

GOVT CHEESE
a memoir

Steven Pressfield

Copyright © 2022 Steven Pressfield

Cover design by Diana Wilburn
All rights reserved
First Sarsaparilla Media Paperback Edition June 2023

For permission to reproduce selections from this book, write to:
Permissions, Sarsaparilla Media LLC
PO Box 2488, Malibu CA 90265

Hardback ISBN: 979-8-9861643-9-7
eBook ISBN: 979-8-9861643-8-0
Audiobook ISBN: 979-8-9861643-5-9
Paperback: ISBN: 979-8-9861643-6-6

Book design by Diana Wilburn

Library of Congress Control Number:
Printed in the United States of America.

www.stevenpressfield.com
9 8 7 6 5 4 3 2 1

for Diana,
who believed in this and willed it into being

I entered [the world of art] without any apparent talent, a thorough novice, incapable, awkward, tongue-tied, almost paralyzed by fear and apprehensiveness. I had to lay one brick on another, set millions of words to paper before writing one real, authentic word dragged up from my own guts. The facility for speech which I possessed was a handicap; I had all the vices of the educated man. I had to learn to think, feel, and see in a totally new fashion, in an uneducated way, in my own way, which is the hardest thing in the world.

Henry Miller, *The Wisdom of the Heart*

IF YOUR ♥ IS NOT IN DIXIE, YOU HAD BETTER GET YOUR 🐴 OUT.

Bumper sticker of the '70s

SIDEBAR #1: A TYPEWRITER

MINE WAS A SMITH-CORONA. I still have it. It's a monster. It weighs twenty-one pounds.

A typewriter is not like a laptop. There's no electrical assist when you hit the keys. You have to pound the hell out of a manual typewriter. Even the sound of an old-school typewriter is violent, the bam, bam, bam of the metal striker bars pounding the paper through an inked ribbon to create the punch-bang impress of a letter and then a word.

A manual typewriter is heavy. No way you can lift it with one hand. It's a two-arm heft, and even then you have to brace the clumsy, ungainly tonnage against your hip or your belly. The machine has to possess mass to hold steady beneath the barrage of the keys being punched and the type bars flying at the paper. The frame is industrial-grade steel like the chassis of a Buick.

I carried my Smith-Corona in the back of my Chevy van for seven years. I never used it. Not once, not even to write a letter. I hated it. My typewriter was a constant reminder of my failure as a husband, as a writer, and as a man. Half a dozen times I came this close to heaving the damn thing out to the alligators. Once in north Georgia, I pulled over in the middle of a bridge. I had the typewriter in both hands at the rail, ready to sling it into the Chattahoochee.

I didn't. I don't know why.

In my van I always stuck my typewriter in the darkest, most remote corner. I was punishing it. Hiding it, hiding my own shame. The worst thing about carrying a type-writer in a vehicle is it keeps rattling. The carriage migrates. Spindly appendages clatter and bang. I finally just stuffed an old T-shirt into the damn thing's innards. I wrapped the machine in a moth-eaten army blanket and wedged it in a rear corner between my spare tire and my tire jack.

Book One

HUGH REAVES

I. VAN LIFE

I drove a van then—a '65 Chevy—with a three-speed manual transmission on the column and an in-line six-cylinder engine.

The van had 27,000 miles on it when I bought it in New York City in 1966. I paid $1,250. The odometer read 374,000 (give or take) when I finally gave it to my friend David in Los Angeles in 1987. A year later it was hauling firewood and sheep dung for his in-laws on the Navajo Reservation in Arizona. It was still running. For all I know, it's running still.

Here's how I had the van set up when I was traveling in it.

I had four heavy plastic milk crates, the kind dairies or supermarkets use to pack twenty-four cartons of milk in. I set each one at a corner of the steel floor of the van. On top of these I balanced my box springs and on top of that went my mattress, which I made up as a bed with sheets and blankets and pillows. The bed filled up the entire interior. I had no room, as with a VW bus, for a table or a stove or a sink. The top of the bed sat at eye-level to the two rear windows and the side windows of the van. I liked that. I could see out at night and not feel claustrophobic.

Underneath the box springs, in the space beneath the elevated milk crates, I slid my clothes (in two cardboard boxes), my tools, tire jack, spare parts, cooking stuff, a cooler, the twenty or thirty paperbacks I was reading at the time, my hated typewriter, and, later—after I found my cat Mo as a kitten on Jacks Peak in Monterey, California—a litter box and a sack or two of kitty litter.

The engine in a '65 Chevy van sits inside, between the two front seats, under a cowling-type cover. The cover gets hot. I had a blanket folded over it for insulation. When I found my cat beside the road that night, the kitten was so tiny he fit easily into the bowl of my two hands. I took him aboard the van and set him down on top of the blanket that covered the engine housing. The surface was soft and toasty. Mo curled into a ball and went immediately to sleep.

The next day I wrote out fifty three-by-five index cards—FOUND KITTEN—with a description and a note of where I'd picked him up. I drove back around the neighborhood, sticking the cards in every mailbox, with my address and phone number at the bottom. I was renting a little house on Pine Street in Pacific Grove then. Three days later nobody had called, so I figured the kitten was mine. He seemed to feel the same way.

Most of this story happened before I found Mo, though.

I'm wondering as I begin this if such a recounting of actual events will be of interest or utility to a reader. People who have read my books, particularly *The War of Art* and its cousins, have a vague idea of the odyssey of a particular solitary guy, wracked by guilt and riven by self-doubt, as he struggles toward his destiny as a writer. But they have only the scantiest conception of the particulars of that journey.

These particulars, I'm hoping, may be of use to others as they wrestle with their own version of that same odyssey.

There can be an element of destiny or fate when such a saga is narrated from back to front. I don't want that. It's misleading. It may throw off another pilgrim on his or her way.

This book, then, is an attempt to tell the true, stupid, blind, gory story in all its stupid, blind, gory details.

It's still about destiny. It's still about meaning. There is very definitely, in my view, an element of fate involved.

But let me try to strip it down.

Let me tell the parts I normally leave out.

We hauled government cheese, dried beans, and powdered milk, among other types of freight, when I worked for a trucking company called Burton Lines in Durham, North Carolina. The year was 1971. I was twenty-eight.

Durham is a tobacco town. The bulk of Burton Lines' business was hauling tobacco. Harold Blackburn, the company's number-one driver, used to say, "'Bacca hauler is the lowest form of life on the American road." He said it proudly.

I'll explain in a few minutes.

I was on my way out of Raleigh/Durham, having given up on finding a job, when the dispatcher at Burton Lines, a former Marine named Hugh Reaves, took a chance and hired me. I had finished a month-long course in tractor-trailer driving a few months earlier, but after at least a hundred tries at other truck lines across the state—Pilot Freight, Overnite, Akers, Estes, Roadway, Carolina Freight, Thurston, Smith's Transfer, etc.—I had to accept the fact that I wasn't going to get on anywhere. I was living with my wife Lesley at her mother's farmhouse in the country outside Raleigh. Lesley and I were taking our last shot at trying to make things work.

I found an interim job delivering institutional foods. I drove a twenty-six-foot, medium-duty refrigerated International with the company name—Monarch Foods—on the side, bringing Simplot crinkle-cut French fries and frozen Salisbury steaks to restaurants, school cafeterias, and so forth. I can't remember what my pay was, but it was well south of a hundred bucks a week. My mother-in-law thought I was a weak, feckless loser. She was fearful for her daughter's future for having linked her fate to mine. To motivate me in my search for better work, my mother-in-law, who was actually a good woman who had been through plenty of tough times herself, used to write on a little blackboard in her kitchen the price of everything she had laid out cash for, that I now owed her. Quart of milk twenty-seven cents, that sort of thing.

My own opinion of myself was lower even than my mother-in-law's. I was totally and utterly ashamed of myself before my wife. It was excruciating just to see her face when she looked at me. A year or so earlier, when she and I had first split up, I worked for a place called Tinsley Oilfield Maintenance in Buras, Louisiana, downriver from New Orleans. It was a bunkhouse operation where all you had to do was show up and they'd put you to work. Every day now at my mother-in-law's farmhouse outside Raleigh, I was thinking, *I'm too ashamed to stay here much longer. If the van will make it to Louisiana, that's where I'm going, and I'll never show my face around here again.*

But back to Monarch Institutional Foods. One morning in November, I was making a delivery to a waffle place called Your House in the Cameron Village shopping center in Raleigh. I hadn't had breakfast and I was hungry. Walking out through the storeroom after the delivery, I helped myself to a 5.5-ounce can of grapefruit juice from the shelf. The manager stopped me. A scene ensued in the rain in the parking lot. Short version—I was fired.

Poor Lesley. I felt so bad for her that she had married a bum like me. I don't remember what either of us said that next morning except that it was still raining and I was on my way to Buras, Louisiana.

But first I stopped at Burton Lines. I had applied twice before and been turned down both times. I don't know why I tried again this time. Burton Lines was located in an unincorporated part of Durham County called Bethesda. I had no idea of this then or later. I was on my way to Highway 70, which I intended to take south to Raleigh to pick up the interstate toward Louisiana. As I drove down Angier Avenue, I thought, *Isn't Burton Lines out here?* I turned left over the railroad tracks onto Ellis Avenue. Coming my way in the rain was one of Burton Lines' GMC Astros, a gray-and-black cabover with its wipers pumping and road spray spewing up beneath its eighteen tires. It passed me and I passed it.

I recognized the terminal, a mile farther on the left. The geography of the lot was this. The dispatcher's office was the first thing you came to on your left, just past the sign:

NO UNAUTHORIZED VEHICLES BEYOND THIS POINT

as you bucked off the two-lane and passed the chain-link fence that bounded the terminal. A group of fuel pumps sat on an elevated island behind a second cyclone fence. You parked in a dirt lot, muddy now in the storm, beside the drivers' and mechanics' cars and pickups. I noticed a camper-shell Ford with a chicken wearing boxing gloves painted on the driver's door. Deeper into the lot, beyond the second chain-link fence, I could see the repair shop, the body and fender bay, and the tall, open-sided shelters with various uncoupled trailers backed under them.

You climbed an outside flight of stairs to the drivers' room and the dispatcher's office. The dispatcher's name, as I said, was Hugh Reaves. His office looked out through high wide windows over the yard and the trucks so he could see everything. Access to Mr. Reaves' office was via a counter-type window, just inside the outer door. Drivers could come up to get their trips, pick up their paychecks, or just to talk to Hugh. A sign said

KEEP THIS COUNTER CLEAN

Mr. Reaves was alone in his office that morning with a desk, filing cabinets, various phones, and so forth behind him.

I came up to the window. I had been a Marine, a reservist. Hugh Reaves still had the buzz cut from his own days as a staff sergeant.

He hired me.

3. A DAY IN THE LIFE

I wake up in my van. I don't know where I am. I don't know who I am. The reality of my existence is that my identity, if I ever had one, has dissolved. Goals. Do I have any? I can't even conceive of the possibility. A purpose? To survive until tomorrow. I open the van's side doors. It's warm. I'm in a dirt turnout at the edge of a farmer's field. Corn. Oh yeah, I'm in Iowa. Where, I have no clue. It takes me a moment to remember where I'm going. East? West? Where am I coming from?

I search around for my jeans and try to open my eyes.

My van is a hive. A rat's nest. This is before I upgraded the status of my bed to include a box springs and actual sheets and blankets. It's just a mattress on the steel floor now. Half a dozen paperbacks litter the blanket I have tossed and twisted into knots along with the plaid-lined Boy Scout sleeping bag somebody gave me in Plaquemines Parish six months ago. My blue jeans and underwear lie in a tangled pile in a rear corner next to my battered sixty-five-cent copy of Jack Kerouac's *On the Road*.

I sit up and rub my eyes. Should I shave? I have no water. Anything to eat? I'm trying to remember what I had last night. Maybe some is still around. Pizza crusts, whatever. Should I pee? Any farmers in the vicinity? Maybe the owner of this land, who might take offense or chase me off?

This is van life for me, circa 1970. I pull on my jeans and step out barefoot into the day. The road is empty. It's a county byway, a farm road. I sought it out last night to get away from any place with traffic. No cars or trucks now. Just my van tucked off beside a fence with a farm tractor churning down a row of corn a thousand yards away.

I move to the day's first big event—peering into the mirror. In Louisiana both my outboard mirrors got torn off by vandals. I have replaced them with oversize, trailer-hauler rear-views. A smart move, actually. You can see for miles in these suckers.

I peer into the glass, hoping my face will have improved overnight. Maybe I have become a different person. Maybe this morning I have some concept of what I'm doing.

No luck.

I'm only twenty-six but I feel fifty.

The best morning I ever had, waking up, was the first day I got to New Orleans about a year ago. I drove into the city late with no clue to local geography. Night had fallen. I didn't want to try to find a room in a strange city after dark, or spend the money either, so I just followed my nose down one street after another, seeking a spot to pull over and sleep. I found a turnoff beyond a cyclone fence down by the waterfront.

I parked and locked the doors, crawled back over the engine into the rear, got under my sleeping covers and corked off. When I woke up, the sun was shining; it was a fine, cheerful day with the smell of the Mississippi coming from the far slope of the levee. I opened the van's side doors. I was parked behind some kind of commercial warehouse. In the seashell-paved lot I saw a couple of parked delivery trucks and guys in workingmen's clothes walking across a creaky loading dock. A sign said:

SOUTHEAST LOUISIANA BANANA COMPANY

I noticed a big iron cage perched at the edge of the loading dock. In the cage was a gorilla. Really. A full-size, live gorilla.

At that moment, a workman came out from the rear of the warehouse. I was sitting in the side door frame of the van with my bare soles on the seashell-paved lot. The workman had two bananas in his hand. He crossed to the gorilla and held out one banana through the bars. The gorilla took it. Then the man came over to me. He gave me the other banana.

The man turned and headed back inside. He never said a word, not to me and not to the gorilla.

The gorilla and I sat there and enjoyed our bananas.

4. AMBITION

I find a place to stay in Durham, about ten minutes from Burton Lines. It's a basement room for twenty-five dollars a month in what I don't realize at the time is a halfway house for people who have recently been released from state mental institutions. Here's what I wrote about that period in *Turning Pro* (2012):

> I wasn't a mental patient myself, but the law of metaphor had brought me to this place as surely as if I had been.
>
> The people in the halfway house were by no means "crazy." They were as interesting and complex a collection of individuals as I had ever met. I made friends. I found a home.
>
> We did a lot of talking in the evenings in the halfway house. We gathered over coffee in the communal kitchen and talked about books and politics and whether aliens were messengers from the future or from God.
>
> I was the only one in the halfway house who had a job. I was making $1.75 an hour at a trucking company, training to become an over-the-road trucker. Everyone else in the halfway house got a check from the state. Social workers appeared from time to time to evaluate the people in the halfway house and to counsel them on their re-integration into society.
>
> I began to wonder how I came to be in this house with these people. Why did I feel so at home? Was this my destiny?

Then one night I had a dream. In the dream I came into my basement room and found that my shirts had all folded themselves in the drawer (instead of being mashed together in their usual jumbled mess.) My boots had crawled out from under the bed where I normally kicked them. They had set themselves upright. They had shined themselves. When I woke up, I thought, "I'm ambitious! I have ambition!"

At the trucking company, I have been assigned by Hugh Reaves to the body-and-fender shop. This will be the first phase in my apprenticeship. My boss in the body shop is a white guy of about fifty named Ernie Beale. Ernie had been a driver for thirty years but a blown-out disc in his lower back has taken him off the road. I'm now his assistant. It's just the two of us. The body shop, like every utility building at the terminal, has an eighteen-foot ceiling to accommodate the trucks that are backed in to be worked on. The roof is corrugated tin. A roll-up door protects the front against rain and snow. The shop has no heat and no air conditioning.

Next to the body shop on one side is the mechanics' area, a double bay with a crew of four. Charley Stewart is the shop chief. Ernie Beale is a really good guy, and so is Charley. Charley had been a stock-car mechanic and a racing driver before that. He's my age, twenty-eight. On the other side of the body shop is the tire bay. Buddy Baldwin, who's the best guy of all, runs this whole area by himself.

Drivers are constantly dinging fenders on their cabs or otherwise banging up their trucks. Ernie's job, and mine now as his apprentice, is to patch them up. That's all we do all day. The body shop universe is one of face masks and paint guns, hardening compound and blower nozzles, Bond-o and power grinders and sandpaper blocks. It's interesting. I like it. At quitting time, Ernie perches on a wooden Nehi case, set upright, and tucks a fresh wad of RED MAN into his jaw. "Another day," he says, "shot." My job is to hose down the bay floor, thumb-streaming into the pit drain the mud clods, the fiberglass dust, the snipped-off rivet ends, the waste triangles of scrap metal, and the rueful lungers of tobacco juice. For the first month, I am not allowed inside a functioning vehicle, except occasionally for my education to ride along downtown with Harold Blackburn or Sammy Hunt, the number one and number two drivers at Burton, when they pick up loads at Liggett & Myers or the American Tobacco Company.

Outside the body-and-fender shop, in an unroofed slot at the south end of the trailer shelter, sits a beat-up old Peterbilt tractor with no roof or fenders or doors, no windshield, and no passenger seat. It's used for switching, i.e., moving trailers around the yard. This is the only vehicle Hugh Reaves will let me touch. His voice crackles with my name at odd hours over the loudspeaker that is mounted on the eave outside his office. I peer out from the body shop toward his big windows overlooking the yard. Hugh Reaves will be pointing at a trailer that another driver has brought in and parked willy-nilly out in the rain. "Get 62B out of this wet." And he gestures through the November drizzle toward an open slot under the shelter.

I think, now, after the dream in the halfway house, *I'm gonna make it here. I'm going to be a driver. I will learn what I have to learn. I will overcome whatever I have to overcome. I'm through being a failure and a loser. I'm going to make it here.*

Have you ever read *Hunger* by Knut Hamsun or George Orwell's *Down and Out in Paris and London*? My story isn't like that. These guys knew they were writers. They were on fire with it. Charles Bukowski is another one. Henry Miller. I would've felt a million times better if I could've imagined I had any talent or a destiny.

I never felt that way for a minute.

I was just a loser trying to crawl out of a hole.

I never wrote to my mother or father during this period. Never wrote to my brother Mike. I was too ashamed. Nor did it occur to me that I might be causing them heartache or anguish by vanishing off the planet. They seemed so far away, I couldn't imagine their lives or anything about them. I certainly couldn't imagine contacting them.

My first writing job was for $150 a week as a junior copywriter for Benton & Bowles at 666 Fifth Avenue in New York. This was straight out of college—and six months in the Marine Corps Reserve—five years before Burton Lines. My boss was a precociously talented writer named Ed Hannibal. One day Ed came in and announced he had written a novel. The book was called *Chocolate Days, Popsicle Weeks*. It was a hit. Overnight Ed became famous. He was a star. He quit the agency to write full time.

I thought, *Shit, I'll do that too. How hard can it b*e?

I quit too.

I will skip over the eighteen months of me trying to write that specific novel, except to say that 99.9 percent of the way through, I choked and blew it up.

Here are a couple of paragraphs from *The Knowledge* (2016). "Tracy" is the fictional version of Lesley:

> Specifics? What difference does it make whether I slept with her sister or her best friend or the nun who prepped her for her First Communion? And the worst part is I did it out of cowardice. Because I didn't have the guts to finish the book that Tracy had dropped out of law school to back me to write. Did I say that was the worst part? No, far crueler was watching Tracy's heart break. Watching her writhe and struggle, with no one to call on but herself, summoning her innermost resources to construct from scratch a self that could survive the blows her worthless husband had delivered upon her. But even that wasn't the cruelest component. More painful still were my attempts at salvage—the forgive-me moments, the I-can-change pleas, the excruciating nightlong talks that only drove my bride and me more deeply into despair. The silk had been torn and nothing could make it whole again.
>
> I had robbed Tracy of everything she had dreamed of for herself and for us as a couple—children, grandchildren, the life we would build together, the prospect of growing old at each other's sides. And the damage didn't stop with me. How would Tracy trust anybody from now on? The next lover? A future husband? I have ruined her life. And nothing I can say or do can ever redeem that.

That was what... three breakups and two try-agains ago? Should I let Lesley know I haven't gone to Louisiana, that I've found work here?

No. It would only upset her.

Leave her alone.

Let her live her life.

6. A HOUSE IN THE COUNTRY

My first paycheck from Burton Lines is $105.45. Fifty bucks has been deducted for a draw Hugh Reaves advanced me to cover my first two weeks. But the remainder is still more money than I've had at one time in the previous four years. The check is drawn on the Wachovia Bank. I take it down to the branch on North Duke Street and cash it. I have no bank account of my own and I feel far too precarious to open one. The service charge for cashing the check is thirty cents.

The first item I buy is socks. There's a flea market every Saturday behind the armory on Polk Street. It takes me an hour to rationalize the forty-nine cents for a six-pack of white tube socks from China, so cheaply made they don't even have a dent for the heel. Another $1.89 and I have two three-packs of white skivvies.

I have to leave the halfway house. Much as I like the people, the place is not good for me. I have a new life now. I have to move on.

I find an abandoned cinder-block house off a two-lane road in the pine woods between Raleigh and Durham. The owner is a widow who owns three other properties. She had no intention of renting this one, she says. It's not fit for human habitation, but she'll let me have it for fifteen dollars a month.

"I'll take it."

The house has no electricity and no running water, no heat, no bathroom, no kitchen. It has a front door but no back door, just an open passage. It has windows but no glass in any of them. The house backs up to a patch of woods—loblolly pines with red clay and pine straw beneath. It has a flat dirt lot on the south side. I park my van and move my box springs and mattress into the house. I bolt together my wooden table and set it up in the kitchen.

My typewriter. I have carried this piece of shit with me through the wars. I have no idea why. Should I bring it inside? I could set it up on the table. It wouldn't be in the way.

I leave it buried under junk in the back of my van.

I move into the house.

7. STEVEN SEAGAL

Twenty-four years later I buy a house in Los Angeles. It's a one-bedroom Spanish-style bungalow off Robertson south of Pico. I'm working on the script for the movie *Above the Law*. One day Steven Seagal comes over. I can't remember why. Probably a script meeting of some kind.

My writing partner—whom I'll call Stanley—is there along with Andy Davis, the movie's director, and two or three ex-cops or small-arms experts who are on hand partly to provide technical expertise but mainly because they just like to hang around Steven Seagal.

Steve makes a call from my phone in the kitchen. Whoever is on the other end of the line apparently asks where he's phoning from.

"Some shithole in East LA," Steve says.

Shithole?

I don't quite see it that way.

Byron Storey is the coolest of the black drivers at Burton Lines. Six in all work here, all hire drivers, meaning they don't own their own trucks but work for a paycheck. About a dozen white drivers fill out the full roster. They work for hire too, except three who own their trucks and drive primarily out of Burton's sister terminal in Reidsville, about fifty miles northwest. Byron is, bar none, the handsomest specimen of male humanity I have ever seen, including Hollywood actors and male models. He knows it but he doesn't make the slightest deal of it.

One afternoon Byron is stricken with an attack of appendicitis. He hits the floor of the drivers' room like he's been shot. An ambulance comes with its siren screaming. Every driver is out in the yard, watching the medics wheel Byron out on a gurney, load him into their wagon, and speed away.

Byron's truck, 324-T, is sitting in the yard bobtail, i.e., without a load. Hugh Reaves eyes me dubiously. "Think you can find American Tobacco downtown and get back in one piece?"

Until that afternoon I had been filling out my logbook each day as "on duty," as Hugh Reaves has insisted, and turning the carbons in to him each Saturday. I have never penciled a page, or even a fifteen-minute increment, as "driving."

"Trip sheet's in Byron's door panel. It's got the address downtown and the trailer number. Fill out the date and time in your own logbook. Here's Byron's lock and key for when you seal the trailer. Park the load in 61A when you get back."

"Then report to you?"

"Yes. Then report to me."

Of every action I have taken from minute one at Burton Lines, the primary terror in my mind, which has never left my thoughts for an instant, is, *Am I going to fuck this up?*

Am I going to steal a 5.5-ounce can of grapefruit juice without thinking about it? Am I going to be late? Am I going to crash a vehicle? Am I going to ruin a repair job?"

I set three wind-up alarms each evening. I get to the yard a half hour before anyone else. I call Hugh Reaves "sir" and do the same to everybody else including Charley Stewart, who's my own age, until they tell me to stop. It's making them feel creepy.

I can't laugh. I can't joke around with the guys. Every step is like tiptoeing across a minefield.

My knuckles are so white maneuvering Byron's 324-T the 4.2 miles along Angier Avenue, turn on Driver Street to East Main and Pettigrew Street, with NC 147 on the left, along Mangum Street until you see the warehouse complex and the hundred-foot-high brick LUCKY STRIKE smokestack visible from Blackwell Street that I'm certain the circulation will never return.

"Where's Byron?" the dock foreman calls to me as I climb down from the cab and, focusing furiously, stride toward him with the load sheet.

"Appendix blew."

"No shit? When?"

"Just now. Hour ago."

"He okay?"

"I think so. The medics took him to the hospital."

The foreman takes my sheet.

"Who're you?"

"Me? I'm nobody."

I have to get my van fixed. It's burning a quart of oil a week. I'm terrified the vehicle will break down some morning on the way to work and Hugh Reaves will fire me. Not to mention the damn thing looks like hell with blue smoke pouring out of the tailpipe, with the muffler itself dangling from a wire coat hanger rigged beneath the chassis. My gas gauge stopped working eighteen months ago. Fuel in the tank? I have to remove the cap, poke a stick in and tug it out to check for depth of dampness. I live in dread of hitting empty some morning on the way to work. My van proclaims, "The individual who drives this is a bum and a loser. He can't get his shit together even to fix the vehicle his life and livelihood depend on."

The South is different from the North and even parts of the West. In the South if something breaks, you don't take it to a mechanic or a repairman. You fix it yourself or you bring it to your buddy or your brother-in-law and he fixes it while in exchange you fix something for him that you know how to do.

Lesley had introduced me to Bruce Simpkins before we split up. Bruce is an auto mechanic, though like so many in this part of the world he has been a stock-car racer and after that a racing mechanic. Bruce is about fifty. He's rail-thin, bald as a turnip, and dressed permanently, it seems, in a set of grease-streaked herringbone Oshkosh coveralls with a thumbed-down Bible in the right-hand cargo pocket. His shop is a corrugated tin shed with a step-down pit instead of a lift at a crossroads called Simpkinsville off NC 96 a few miles north of Zebulon. Bruce's cousin owns the country store across the way. His mother runs the timber operation—for paper, not lumber—that extends for another mile south along the two-lane. Simpkins forebears go back to Chancellorsville and Antietam and no doubt a hundred years before that.

"She needs rings," Bruce tells me.

Piston rings. "That means pulling the head, doesn't it?"

"It means valves and tappets too. I can grind and fill what you got, save you a little. Maybe bore the cylinders out."

I ask how much.

"Three hundred."

"Can I pay fifty at a time?"

"I'll let you have my Ford while I'm working on her. But I got three other vehicles ahead of you."

Bruce has invited me to church. I've attended with him four times, going back to before I started working at Burton Lines.

"Not a church really." That's Bruce's original description. "More of a fellowship."

I meet him again this Sunday. He and several like-minded souls have taken over an abandoned house off a country road without a name and fixed it up, or at least cleared the trash and junked cars out of the yard. The group of about a dozen meets in what had been the living room. They don't have any chairs, so each person brings his or her own.

If there ever was a sincere congress of souls, this is it. The brothers and sisters share their inner anguish with heartbreaking candor and are greeted with love from their fellows in such depth it shames me just to be present and privy. And all of it is wrapped in such humility it cannot be witnessed without fighting tears.

Bruce stands. He's wearing a white cotton shirt with a starched collar and a pocket protector that holds seven or eight pens and pencils. The bulb end of a tire pressure gauge peeks from one corner. Bruce's black cotton trousers, worn to a shine through the seat, hang on his lanky frame like rags on a scarecrow. He clutches his even-more-weathered

King James Bible in both hands. He is offering his testimony, as any may at any time in the fellowship. It's December and raining. A raw wind works through the cracks around the windows and the half-open (so latecomers will feel welcome) front door.

"Daytime," Bruce says, "I can get by. I got my tricks. But nights? Nights is different."

He talks about feelings of shame and despair and self-hatred coming over him so strong, night after night, that he shakes like a jack pine in a gale. "Bones rattling, hands quaking... I can hear my teeth chattering in my skull."

Bruce recounts one terrible night, falling to his knees and begging the Lord for surcease from this torment. Out loud, Bruce says, he acknowledges all his sins (though for the life of me, listening, I can't imagine what these infractions might be, Bruce being such a good, honorable man).

"Like that, a peace come over me... a peace that passeth all understanding. I laid me down and went to sleep like a child."

When he awoke, Bruce says, he had a vision of this house, this derelict structure that he had driven past a thousand times. He knew of a sudden that the Lord intended it for a place of worship, a fellowship where anybody could come to pray or sing or do nothing at all but just be with brothers and sisters seeking peace.

What good people! What kind hearts! My own suspicious vision scans the room, person by person, seeking any sign of falseness or insincerity, some angle or scheme. I find none. Every soul beneath this roof, perched on their lawn chairs and kitchen seats brought from home, has been split apart at the core. No one has any agenda except release from pain.

I try as hard as I can to be like these good people, to be like Bruce. I read the Biblical passages he tells me to. Many make me weep, as they come from such a place of depth and compassion. I keep hoping and even praying that Jesus will be the answer for me. But I can't make that final leap. I believe in Bruce, though. Nothing can change that. We sit on soft-drink cases beside the pot-belly stove in his shop, drinking coffee, and he tells me about his days driving the circuit, drinking and chasing women, always with a rueful shake of the head.

"You can come work for me," Bruce says, "if you get tired of driving up and down the highway. Don't worry if you don't know nothing. I'll teach you."

I thank Bruce and tell him I'm happy at Burton Lines. It's exactly the work I want.

"If I can just make it stick," I say. "If I can just make it stick."

Tobacco in leaf form is trucked in hogsheads. A hogshead is like a gigantic barrel. Coopers make them. They're oak with iron bands around the rims and waists. A full hogshead weighs a thousand pounds. Huck Finn's father slept in a hogshead. That's how big they are.

The Liggett & Myers and American Tobacco Company warehouses in downtown Durham are made for trucks to drive into. Not to an exterior loading dock. All the way inside. That's how you take on a load of hogsheads.

You enter up a ramp wide enough to accommodate two tractor-trailers abreast. Open your nose. The sweet, tobacco smell permeates everything. It overpowers even the diesel stink thrumming from the double stacks of Harold Blackburn's 304-T and the five other trucks from other companies idling beneath the thirty-foot-high ceilings. A rich, earth-spawned tang oozes from the stained, hundred-year-old American elm columns that support the roof. The stink is in the bricks, it's in the walls, in your hair, under your fingernails. It's a great smell. It's alive.

Here's how you'd take on a load of tobacco in hogsheads.

You pull the truck in among the towering rows stacked eight hogsheads-high to the ceiling. Forklifts with extra-long extenders zig and zag across the dark, tobacco-stained floor, grabbing the oversized barrels off the summits of the piles and scooting them over to your truck. The trucks are flatbeds, not box trailers. Thirty-six hogsheads make a load, in nine rows of four. Hugh Reaves sends me as a ride-along with Harold, Sammy, or Byron, so I can watch and be watched over. The first two hogsheads are set in place by the forklift driver, side by side at the very front of the trailer, against the steel forewall. Six-foot timber braces, with notches like oversize Lincoln logs, go on top of this first pair of hogsheads to form a floor for the second row. You, the driver, must wrangle these. You're in coveralls and gloves because the tobacco grit will work its way into every pore unless you're protected.

As soon as the first two-atop-two hogsheads are in place, your job is to lash them down with chains and binders. You work fast because the forklift drivers are bringing the next set of four. You clamber up the load like a mahout on an elephant, dragging the heavy chain that'll tie down the row. Along the flank of the flatbed runs a horizontal steel rail. The binders have hooks that seat into this. You thread the chain through a block-and-tackle whose terminus holds a heavy steel lever. You crank this to ratchet the chain down tight, lashing the first row of hogsheads in place.

Nine rows later you've got a load and they're all snugged down tight and ready to roll. Except for me with my tendency to unconsciously sabotage myself. I'm focusing furiously, double- and triple-checking each linkage, terrified that I will fail to seat a binder properly or lock down a chain and the whole load will come toppling off at the first turn on the road. I don't know how Harold senses this about me, but he does. He is a great mentor because he never gets mad or impatient. He isn't a taskmaster; he just does his job without haste and with solid professionalism. If I have left excess slack in a chain, he'll tug on it, just enough to show me I haven't ratcheted the binders tightly enough. "These sonsofbitches'll come a-loose on you. Y'ever wanna see a mess, son, see that."

Harold instructs me on driving beneath railroad bridges and highway overpasses. "Know the clearance of every overhead you come to. Know where the top of your load is at all times."

By now Harold has his load. The forklift operators are waving us to clear out. Other trucks are outside waiting. The last thing the lift guys do is load Harold's weather covers, which he has brought from the terminal lashed to the deck of the flatbed—three of them, waterproof, one about forty pounds, the others about seventy, too heavy to wrangle by hand—onto the top of the load. Harold and I will cover the load when we get back to the yard.

11. DR. JEFF

I had another job before I went to the trucking school. I worked for a physician named Jeffrey Winograd—"Dr. Jeff." Doctor Jeff had his own one-story, red-brick medical building on a country road between Wendell and Zebulon. I had come down with an eye infection when I first got to North Carolina with Lesley. We were living at her mother's farmhouse. Dr. Jeff had billboards on the highway that said ALL WELCOME.

I went. It was noon on a Saturday. The doctor and I were the only white people in the building. We got to talking. Dr. Jeff was from New Rochelle, New York. This was the site, I told him, where I had enlisted in the Marine Corps Reserve. He knew the armory. "On the Post Road, just south of Salesian High?"

I told him my aim was to get on somewhere as a trucker, but I needed money first to go to a driving school.

"What would you think," Dr. Jeff said, "about working for me?"

There was a crossroads south of the hamlet of Lizard Lick with a self-pay gas-dispensing station. Three pumps, no attendant. The brand name, on a big orange sign said

HEP-UR-SEF

You put quarters in a slot and the pumps dispensed your gas. This was the first of the self-serve stations. There was nothing like it anywhere.

Dr. Jeff had a corrugated-tin storage shed on the entry drive to the station. You drove past it on your way to the pumps. "We'll clean it up and make it an office for you."

He had the front painted and a desk and file cabinets put in. Outside he hung a shingle

DR. JEFF MEDICAL ANNEX ALL WELCOME

The shingle had a cartoon drawing of Dr. Jeff with a lab coat, a stethoscope, and a little patch of thinning hair.

My job was to sit behind the desk and steer anybody who came in to Dr. Jeff. I would make an appointment or drive them over myself if they needed help right away. Rich or poor, insured or uninsured, the doctor turned nobody away. It was all on some program from the state.

I told Dr. Jeff I felt guilty about the framed medical diplomas he had hung on the wall behind my desk. Dr. Jeff's degree was from Vanderbilt. Uncle Sam had paid his way. He had served his hitch in WestPac—Vietnam—and had come home determined to launch his civilian practice on his own terms. "Don't worry about the diplomas. Half the folks who'll come through those doors can't read anyway."

I worked for Dr. Jeff for four months. Twice I had men come in bleeding from the rectum. Neither was accompanied. Both had driven themselves and refused to let me drive them to the medical building. Both got back in their trucks and went there on their own.

At first only the odd drive-by showed up at the annex. A farmer in an ancient pickup would poke his head in, or a mom dragging three kids would appear on foot. I was reading *Siddhartha* and *The Moviegoer*. I'd set the paperbacks aside when a customer appeared. I had been terrified that I would be called upon to offer actual services or, God forbid, diagnose somebody. I never had to. People would tell me themselves what ailed them. Sometimes they'd tell me for hours.

Have you heard of a prolapsed uterus? I never imagined the condition was so widespread. With advanced age or simply ill health or malnutrition, the intestinal wall loses the strength to contain the reproductive organs. The deflated sack of the uterus literally falls out. The women themselves showed me how to push it back in.

Kids came in with bellies distended from hunger. Men stopped to borrow money for gas. People showed up with burns or bunions or wicked-looking boils on the ankles and shins. I never knew toes could grow in such grotesque shapes or that the soles, even of little children, could be riven with such pustules and lesions. My heart broke each time the door creaked open. The burns were often in the form of circles, blistered in patterns on the chest or back. Witch doctoring. People came in emaciated with pinworms and tapeworms. My primary job was to load them into my van and drive them over to Dr. Jeff's.

Six years later, in Washington State, a friend and I helped another man who was bleeding from the anus. My friend said, "He's gone." The bleeding man knew it. You could see in his eyes the same mute acceptance of his fate that I saw over and over in the people who trooped through the door that said ALL WELCOME.

An inspector from Raleigh came by one day and shut the annex down. He looked about twenty, with a white shirt and lace-up shoes, driving a gunmetal-gray Plymouth Satellite. He had me follow him in the van over to Dr. Jeff's medical building.

"I'm not gonna cite you, Dr. Winograd," he told Jeff with a glance over his shoulder as if he expected some supervisor to overhear him. "But y'all can't keep doing this. If somebody dies..."

Dr. Jeff cut me loose with three hundred bucks in twenties.

That paid for my month at the tractor-trailer driving school.

I have made a friend. Here's what I wrote about him in *Turning Pro* (2012):

> There was a redheaded cat who used to come around sometimes when I lived in that house in the country. He was a battle-scarred old tom who lived in the woods. On nights when I was home, I would cook supper over a little campfire out back. The cat would materialize and sit across from me while I ate. I tried to toss him scraps of hamburger or hot dogs from time to time, but he wouldn't take them. He was nobody's pet.
>
> The geography of our dinners together was that I would sit on the cinderblock step at the back of the house. The fire was in front of me inside a circle of stones on a patch of grass. The woods started ten feet away. The redheaded cat would sit at the edge of the woods, facing me. He didn't lie down. He sat up, facing me, with his big front paws beneath him.
>
> The cat regarded me with an expression that was somewhere between condescension and disdain. There was no doubt in either of our minds which one of us was the superior being or which one possessed self-command and self-sovereignty. There was no doubt which one could take care of himself and which one had his shit together. That cat looked at me as if he was deciding whether or not to kick my ass.

I admired that redheaded cat. He became a role model for me. I wanted to be like that redheaded cat. I missed him when he didn't show up.

I regarded the apparition of that redheaded cat as a good omen and a sign that, maybe, I was on the right path.

People think because over-the-road tractor-trailers are so big that they have massive powerplants. They don't. You can't make an engine big enough to handle forty thousand pounds of payload and twenty-eight thousand pounds of pulling vehicle.

"First thing," Harold says. "Don't never use the clutch. Don't need it."

To watch a skilled driver go through the gears on a tractor-trailer is like listening to music. There's no clanging or lurching, no gaps in the smooth application of power. I'm watching Harold's right hand on the shift knob as we head north on the interstate. The throw from one gear to the next is two inches, maybe less. I can barely see Harold's hand move, that's how smooth it is. He's not even thinking. He's part of the truck.

When it's my turn, Harold watches me. My experience, other than switching trailers around the terminal, is entirely from the driving school. My left foot works the clutch the way they taught us there.

"Don't be scared," Harold says. "The gearbox ain't gonna blow up."

He makes me try shifting without the clutch on a level stretch. We're approaching Petersburg, Virginia, on I-95.

"You're in ninth now," Harold says. "Take her to the top. Feel the engine maxing out? She wants to upshift. Sense for the gap to open. Shift when you feel it. Don't touch the clutch."

The engine on a tractor-trailer has a governor. It tops out at thirty-five hundred rpm. You can't make the powerplant rev higher no matter how hard you stand on the accelerator. "When the tach hits thirty-five hundred in any gear," Harold says, "the transmission wants to upshift. Hear her whining? She wants you to swap cogs."

He instructs me to press gently on the shift knob toward the point where it comes out of gear and slides into neutral. "Take out the slack. Press against the wall. That's it. Feel her release? Go now!"

Everything is double-clutch in a tractor-trailer. There's no synchromesh. To shift from one gear to another, you come out of that gear and into neutral, hold for a beat, then shift into the next gear. What's happening is in neutral the transmission is engaged, meaning the gearbox is synched to the wheels on the road. If you're upshifting from seventh to eighth, say, when you slip into neutral, the transmission RPMs immediately drop. Wait for them to fall five hundred. It takes less than a second. "Don't watch the tach. Just listen. Hear where she wants to shift?"

Come out of neutral into eighth.

"That's it. You did it. Didn't need no clutch at all, did you?"

The engine in a tractor-trailer, Harold is saying, has an "operating range." The operating range is the spread of RPMs—between three thousand and thirty-five hundred—within which the diesel delivers maximum effective torque.

"Don't never, never, let your revs get out of the operating range. From the moment you shift out of first leaving the yard till the moment you shut down at the delivery dock, that needle should never stray out of the box."

It's two in the morning, passing the Bermuda Hundred exit. The interstate has ascents and descents here. Harold has me practice between tenth and eighth.

"Downshift's the opposite. Feel it on this uphill? You're climbing in tenth. Hear the engine start to lug? She's straining. RPMs dropping. The engine don't have enough power on this grade to keep her at this speed in that gear. Wait till the tach falls to three thousand..."

I dart my eyes to the panel.

"Don't look," says Harold. "Just listen You'll hear it. Come into neutral for half a beat. Now bring the revs up. Come up five hundred, to the top, to the redline. You'll feel it. Now she wants to shift down, to the next lower gear. Hit it!

"You'll get the hang," Harold says. "Just takes a little practice."

Harold is dark-haired, muscular, about forty. He's wearing black half-boots, black work pants, and a white Western shirt. He looks a bit like Ernie Kovacs—the same mustache, same shiny hair spilling down over his forehead, He is without question the number one at Burton Lines.

Harold has noticed my Louisiana license plates. "Two good things about Louisiana," he says now. "Phone calls for a nickel and license tags good for two years."

Harold tells me he asked Hugh Reaves to let me ride along with him on this trip. "I can see you're ready. Hugh's too hard on you. He needs to let you get on."

Harold tells me that this trip—Durham to Ancram, New York—is the perfect one to learn on. "It's long enough, twelve hundred miles total, so you get the feel of an over-the-road trip. We'll deliver one load and pick up another. The route's got interstates, country roads, city driving. It's a night trip so you get to work in the dark. Hugh wanted me to be the one to take you, too. Report back to him." Harold grins. "Don't worry. You're doing fine."

Harold has me pull in at a truck stop north of Petersburg. He directs me to bypass the fuel pumps. Burton has satellite and affiliated terminals up and down the East Coast and over the mountains into Kentucky, West Virginia, and Tennessee. "We'll top off the tanks at one of them stops. Why pay interstate rates?"

I cross at Harold's side to the truck stop café. How lucky am I to have found two such great guys as Hugh Reaves and Harold? What they're giving me is beyond price. I can see Harold has set his own ego aside completely. As we roll north and he tells stories, it's all for me, for my education, to help me calm down, to gain confidence.

"Haulin' 'bacca's the dirtiest job in the trucking industry. You know it yourself from what we done, just to tie down a load of hogsheads. And that's our cleanest loads. Pipe? Wait till you try hauling that. Fertilizer? Junked cars? Cardboard trash? But I tell you what, son. Burton Lines is always gonna be in business. When you feed off the bottom, there's never no shortage of work."

In the café, Harold orders coffee and pie. "Never eat a straight-up meal when you're driving. All the blood goes to your belly for digestion. Makes you sleepy." I absorb this gravely. "Sleeping and eating's just habits," Harold says. "No real need for either."

Outside, crossing between the towering rows of parked and idling diesels, Harold points out the drivers from the big dry-freight outfits like Carolina Freight, Akers, and Overnite. Their trousers are dry-cleaned, he says. "See the creases? See the shine on their shoes? These boys don't never touch a load like you and me. Their trailers are sealed before they even get to the terminal. All they do is climb aboard and drive."

On the road again, Harold takes the wheel. He asks me where I'm living. I tell him I've got a little house where they're building the Research Triangle. Harold tells me he's on Angier Avenue, just past the Emanuel Apostolic Church. He's got a wife and two kids, a girl and a boy. It's his second marriage, Harold says. His wife's name is Shirley. "Come for dinner. You'll meet her." He laughs. "She tamed me."

Harold raises fighting chickens. That was his Ford pickup I noticed in the parking lot the first morning with the rooster wearing boxing gloves on the driver's door. Harold explains that he doesn't actually fight the chickens, meaning train them and put them into the ring. He just raises them till they're old enough to be sold at auction. "Fighting chickens got bloodlines like thoroughbred racehorses. Got papers. You wouldn't believe what a bird with a prime bloodline goes for."

He tells me a little about Hugh Reaves. "Hugh made this company.

He is this company. You look at the drivers in that room. Black or white, none better. But each one has screwed up at some point before they came here—with the law or with their own craziness. Hugh took 'em on when nobody else would. And he's stuck by every one."

I ask Harold why he doesn't drive for Carolina or Pilot Freight or one of the top-shelf lines that would pay him triple what he makes at Burton.

"I wouldn't have 'em and they wouldn't have me. I'm too colorful. You know what them big outfits are looking for in a driver? Someone with bank loans and debts, someone in over their head with kids, boats, and mortgages... someone too scared and too ass-deep in hock to do anything but toe the line."

By the time we pass the Thomas Edison rest stop on the New Jersey Turnpike I'm behind the wheel again and Harold is talking about women. "There's two kinds of females in this world." He's got his boots off and his stocking feet up on the bare-metal dash. "Ones you love and ones you love like crazy."

Harold tells me about his first wife, Darla. "I went to jail over her. Twice. There was times," he says, "too many to remember, when I'd find myself down on my knees, praying to heaven to release me from the spell she had over me.

"Before her," Harold says, "I'd never been with a woman I couldn't control. They were the ones that wanted me. I was the one in charge. Not with Darla. I was the one peering through the peephole. She turned me inside-out and upside-down. She knew it. She loved it. And the more power she had over me, the crazier I got about her."

Harold glances across to see if I have any idea what he's talking about.

"And the strangest part was, when I was with her, it wasn't that good. Sex? I've been with woman after woman that was ten times better. Half the time I didn't even like her! But she had me like a wolf in a trap. Away from her, I was out of my mind. Sleep? No chance! My mind would just run away with itself. This went on for years. Years."

Harold instructs me to stay on 95 past Elizabeth, looking for the exit onto I-80 just past Teterboro.

He shakes his head, remembering Darla. "Finally one evening, I'm meeting her for supper at a place called the Statehouse Grill in Raleigh. I get there a few minutes early, so I'm sitting in the Ford having a smoke when she turns the corner, about a hundred feet down the street, and comes walking this-a-way on the sidewalk. She hasn't seen me yet. It's one of them moments when you get to look at a person you know, just for a heartbeat, with fresh eyes, like you've never seen 'em before.

"I see my wife's long legs swishing beneath that skirt, see her hips swing the way they do. It's summer and her arms are bare and tanned. I can see how pretty she is, and how any man on the street would want her. Then it hits me.

"I'm not in love with her no more."

Harold glances to me. "Just like that," he says. "The spell's broke."

He shakes his head, remembering.

"That terrible aching feeling is gone. My heart feels like a thousand-pound weight has been lifted off it. Thank you, Jesus!" Harold turns toward me. "Y'ever felt that way, brother?"

I tell him I know the crazy part. I haven't felt the spell-breaking part.

Harold laughs and turns back to the road.

"Two kinds of women," he says. "Ones you love and ones you love like crazy."

After a month and a half in the body shop, my duties are expanded. Hugh Reaves assigns me to help Buddy Baldwin with the tires. The tire bay is next door to the body shop, under the same roof with the same eighteen-foot roll-up doors that face onto the unpaved lot. My job is basically to help Buddy unload the retreads that come in twice a week on the Bandag truck. That, and pull out and back-in whatever truck or trailer Buddy happens to be working on.

I see Harold's 304-T as it pulls in and out on various trips. But Hugh Reaves doesn't send me out with him again. Nor with Sammy or Byron. He does begin dispatching me when I'm not working tires with Buddy or applying Bond-o with Ernie to pick up loads of hogsheads for other drivers downtown at American Tobacco or Liggett & Myers. I learn the back route to Pettigrew Street, Mangum, and Blackwell without swimming through the traffic on East Main and how to navigate the jams when the various factory shifts let out. I drive the loads back to the terminal, cover them and park them under the shelters for the other drivers to pick up. But I never get to deliver an actual load.

When Harold or Byron or Sammy or any of the others return from a trip, I wash and fuel their tractors, check their tires, and look to repair any dings or tend to any service items that need to be taken care of. When we need parts, I cannibalize them from the half-dozen wrecks that squat in the weeds alongside mounds of tire casings, spent batteries, busted fenders, and junked windshields and mirrors in the unofficial scrapyard behind the trailer shelters.

It has become my job as well to arrive at the shop an hour before the mechanics or Buddy or Ernie. I sweep up, put the coffee on, and make sure there's toilet paper in the two bathrooms as well as paper towels in the dispensers. If the morning is cold, I fire up the space heaters. The shop guys kick in a buck each day to an old Valvoline can that sits on the shelf above the air compressor. This becomes a pool from which I buy donuts, sugar, creamer, etc.

There's a half-wrecked tractor languishing among the cattails and derelict vehicles at the very back of the yard. Its number is 306-T. Hugh Reaves decides to spare it when the salvage guys come buying scrap metal. "I think we can save this sonofabitch."

Burton's trucks are all GMC Astros. They're cab-overs, meaning there's no big long hood out front. Their faces are flat. The cab is square. The powerplant—a Cummins N-series diesel—sits beneath the cab, on the centerline behind the seats. For the mechanics to get at it, they have to tilt the entire cab forward—doors and windshield, roof, steering column and all.

The tractor bodies themselves are steel and fiberglass. It takes Ernie a week to patch and paint 306-T into something resembling a respectable vehicle. An uncracked windshield comes from a different junked Astro, a set of outboard mirrors from a third. Burton's colors are black and gray. Ernie and I work masking tape and stencils to apply the company logo to the cab facing and to both doors. From the office come the various decals and DOT-required safety stickers. Buddy replaces all ten tires. Charley Stewart and the mechanics rebuild the engine.

I go to lunch with Buddy and Charley one day. The bumper sticker on Charley's '62 Ford pickup says:

ANTI-SMOKING PROPAGANDA MAY
BE HAZARDOUS TO YOUR ECONOMIC HEALTH.

Normally I would wolf a wax-paper lunch of sliced bologna and

Velveeta on Holsum bread with Miracle Whip out back by myself or maybe make a quick run for hot dogs at Amos n' Andy's #3 on Leggett Street but this day for some reason Charley says let's get out into the country. We drive to the house of a black family Buddy knows. We enter through a back door into the big kitchen. Half a dozen mismatched tables fill the patched linoleum space. Working men, black and white, are digging into plates of fried chicken or country ham with collard greens, black-eyed peas, fried okra, and sopping up the juice with hush puppies. Five-gallon pots of various stews and bean dishes simmer on the three side-by-side stoves. There's no menu or table service and no checks. You just point. When it comes time to pay, one of the ladies tells you how much. Our three heaping plates together come to $1.45.

As Charley, Buddy, and I are getting up to leave, a white man steps up before me grinning. It's Dr. Jeff. I shake his hand and make intros.

"My tenure as Dr. Jeff is over," my former boss says. He tells me he's taken a job at Duke University Hospital as an ER doc. "I'm Dr. Winograd now."

Dr. Jeff is also engaged. He's buying a house in Cary. I congratulate him. He doesn't look quite as happy as he's letting on to be. "Look at you," Dr. Jeff says. "You got your wish. Good luck to you."

On the ride back I fill Charley and Buddy in on who Dr. Jeff is and how I know him. "What'd he mean," Buddy asks, "when he said you got your wish."

"To drive," I say.

It's another week before the gaskets arrive for 306-T so Charley can install the rebuilt injectors. The final item is a remanufactured Road Ranger transmission. It's five-thirty, quitting time, before the last mechanical check is completed. Charley asks me to stick around in case Hugh Reaves needs any last paperwork for the state. Charley performs the road test on 306-T himself, coupling to a box trailer and taking the full rig out Angier Avenue via NC 70 and up onto the interstate. He's gone most of an hour. When he gets back, he pulls the truck into the shop where he says he'll make a few final fixes before he calls it a night. Ernie is still there and so is Buddy.

306-T gleams under the overhead lights. I have to admire the rebuild job all hands have done.

"What you think?" Charley asks me, indicating the truck.

"About what?"

Charley cocks his head with a light in his eye.

"Who you think this damn thing's for, son?"

15. WINN-DIXIE

Across from the North Hills Mall in Raleigh is a smaller plaza with a Winn-Dixie. I park the van and dash in. I have delivered six loads so far in 306-T without mishap. Another is waiting under the shelter at the terminal now. I've made this quick sprint into town to update my proof of residency for the DMV. I want to pick up some sandwich fixings, donuts, and milk before I head back. It's one in the afternoon on a rainy, frozen day forty-eight hours short of Christmas.

As I grab a cart and start toward the cold cuts section, I spot Lesley. She's with a guy. She hasn't seen me.

My heart rate leaps. Before I realize what I'm doing, I have ditched my cart and ducked from sight into the bread and pastry aisle. I flee via the rear delivery docks with my chest pounding and have to take such a wide great-circle route around the store that I'm soaked through by the time I get back to my van in the front parking lot. I'm home at two fifteen feeling like a complete coward. The cupboard is bare.

The load that's waiting under the shelter at the terminal is twenty textile manufacturing machines from a bankrupt mill in Cooleemee in Davie County, weighing forty thousand pounds according to the bill of lading. The contraptions are so spindly and top-heavy their footings have been literally hammered into the trailer's pine floor with ten-penny nails. The load is bound for the J.P. Stevens warehouse in Reidsville. The trip will take an hour and a half at the most. Delivery is slated for seven tomorrow morning. I had intended to let the storm blow over and leave sometime around four in the morning.

Fuck it.

I head to the lot and start off now.

Durham to Reidsville is ninety miles via the two-lane 501 North to Roxboro and 158 East after that. Rain has stopped. I pull into the Stevens lot just as the sun is sinking past the tops of the bare maples west of the warehouse. The place is still brightly lit and bustling. It'll be accepting loads for another hour.

The factory dock has six bays. Every slot is taken, "Drop your trailer out yonder beside them others on that pad," says the supervisor. He points to a concrete hardstand about a hundred yards out. Several other trailers sit there.

The way you drop a trailer is you park it first on the spot you want to leave it. In this case, I back it in between two other trailers on the concrete pad. I dismount from the cab and walk straight back past the saddle tanks. On the left side of the trailer, tucked beneath, sits a folding hand-crank. The crank lowers two heavy steel legs from beneath the front end of the trailer.

I unfold the crank and start grinding. The steel legs lower slowly. Each has a wide steel footplate. When the plates reach the ground, the crank resists, like a screwdriver when you've turned a screw as far as it'll go. The legs have now taken the weight of the trailer. The trailer is perched firm and stable, no longer dependent on the horizontal "fifth wheel" at the rear of the tractor to hold its front end up. I crank it a half-inch higher, just to give myself a tad of extra clearance when I pull forward and out from under.

I set the folding crank handle back into its carrying cradle beneath the trailer and push in the telescoping shaft, out of the way. Standing tight against the flank of the trailer, I reach my right hand in and under toward a steel handle beneath the trailer. I grab it. The handle releases the yoke that secures the kingpin on the bottom of the trailer to the flat, horizontal "fifth wheel" at the rear of the tractor. I pull hard on the handle. I can hear and feel the yoke release.

I'm now uncoupled. I'm concentrating hard, making sure I don't miss any steps. Legs down. Yoke released. I can pull the tractor out now from beneath the trailer and the trailer will stay in place, supported by the rear eight wheels and the two front legs I have just cranked down. In this case, tonight, when all the spaces at the loading dock are occupied, the trailer may sit for a few minutes or even a few hours before a switching unit—basically a yard tractor—is sent out by the dock supervisor to pick up the trailer and back it in to a then-open space on the dock.

I'm good. Not thinking about Lesley anymore. I make one final check.

My trailer is unhooked and parked. I've pulled out from beneath it. Nothing has gone wrong. All that's left is to get my papers signed and bobtail home.

But as I cross on foot toward the loading dock, I see a truck pull out. A space has opened. The supervisor whistles. "Hey, Burton! Back your trailer in. Take this slot!"

He waves to me to re-couple and deliver my load.

I trot back to 306-T and climb aboard. I back in under my trailer, hop out, and re-crank the support legs up. The full weight of the trailer settles now onto the flat of the tractor's "fifth wheel." I climb back into the cab. Air pressure's good. Check my mirrors. Check right and left for trucks in motion. All clear. Release the parking brake. Shift into first. Start forward...

Suddenly I feel the cab lurch. A sound like an airplane crashing booms from eight feet behind me. I hit the brakes in panic and peer into the mirrors...

My trailer, loaded with forty thousand pounds of frail, spindly textile equipment, has crashed forward to the ground like a camel shot to its knees.

Around the yard, drivers and warehousemen are staring. The sun is setting. Dark is coming.

I stare helplessly at the wreck. I know exactly what has gone wrong.

I failed to re-yoke the fifth wheel to the kingpin when I pulled out. When I got into the cab to re-couple, I should have backed against the weight of the stationary trailer until I heard the clanging sound of the yoke as it set back into place around the kingpin. Then I would have been recoupled. Instead, I backed only part way under. The weight of the trailer had formed a half-assed connection, resting on the "fifth wheel." But the yoke had never set shut.

As 306-T rolled forward, it pulled out from under the trailer. The trailer crashed nose-first onto the concrete.

I'm standing now in the deepening gloom, staring at my crumpled, heeled-over trailer full of top-heavy manufacturing equipment that must be worth several hundred thousand dollars and has no doubt crashed and jumbled all over itself. What can I do? There's no way to right this mess without a massive crane.

"Better call this in, son," says the dock supervisor. He lets me use the phone on his desk to call Hugh Reaves.

I feel about six inches tall as I explain the situation. Hugh Reaves doesn't get mad. "I'll send someone to help you. Sit tight." And he hangs up.

The drivers and warehousemen do their best, for a minute or two, to make me feel like I'm not the first to dump a load on its face. But this is different for me. These are my demons. This is me. This is the shit I do, no matter how hard I try to stop myself.

Byron, the handsome black driver who had the appendectomy,

comes out to rescue me. Three hours have passed. It's pitch dark. A small mound of Marlboro butts has collected at my feet.

What have I expected in terms of salvage equipment? A twenty-ton truck wrecker? A crane? Byron has come out from home, leaving his dinner, ninety miles in his own pickup. He carries nothing but a heavy-duty hand jack and a stack of six-inch-thick wooden blocks, each about eighteen inches square. "Stand yonder," Byron directs me. "Crank the trailer legs down as I go."

He sets the jack beneath the frame under the trailer and inserts blocks of wood, one on top of another, between the jack plate and the bottom of the trailer. He starts pumping. By hand. To my astonishment the jack, a quarter inch at a time, lifts the trailer and its forty thousand pounds of load. As each increment of height appears, I crank down the trailer legs to take the weight.

Byron gets it to height. He climbs into the cab, backs 306-T under, and yokes the fifth wheel.

"Go on," he says, stepping down. "Take her in to the dock."

17. AMOS 'N ANDY'S

Two lunchtimes after the incident with the trailer, Hugh Reaves calls me into his office. "Let's you and me go someplace where we can talk."

I get into the passenger seat of his Chrysler LeBaron. Hugh Reaves drives to Amos 'n Andy's #5 out on the Raleigh bypass. He parks. We go in. I note a bumper sticker on a pickup as we pass:

IF YOUR♥IS NOT IN DIXIE,
YOU HAD BETTER GET YOUR🐴 OUT.

Amos 'n Andy's sells nothing but hot dogs. You can't get anything else. "How many?" says the counterman when we enter. Hugh Reaves orders two. I've lost all appetite but I hold up two fingers just the same. The counterman dishes both orders, in paper wrappers, in under ten seconds. Mr. Reaves leads us to a booth in a back corner.

"What's wrong with you, son? I took a chance on you."

I apologize abjectly for the incident with the textile machinery. I'll pay for it. I'll settle what I owe if it takes ten years.

"Insurance covers the damages," says Hugh Reaves, "which, by the way, weren't half as bad as they ought to have been. But it doesn't pay for Byron's time or my heartburn. And it won't pay the next time you pull this shit."

He studies me for a long moment.

"I don't know what your story is, son, and I don't wanna know. I can see you're working something out in your life. I can see you're trying your best. I can cut you slack. I'm trying to. But there's one thing you have to understand."

Hugh Reaves pauses and meets my eye.

"Burton Lines," he says, "is *a commercial enterprise designed to make money*. This is a business. A business *you work for*.

"When I give you a load, I expect you to deliver it—on time and intact, just like Harold and Sammy and Byron and everyone else who drives for this company. Are you listening to me? Is what I'm saying sinking in?"

"Yes, sir."

"You're here to drive, understand? Nothing else. You're a professional. Your job is to deliver loads. That's what Burton Lines pays you to do. That's what I pay you to do. Do you understand?"

"I do, sir."

"I hired you because you were a Marine. That's the only goddam reason I took you on."

"I understand, sir."

"Do you? Cause you sure as shit don't look like it."

18. THREE DAYS OF PEACE AND MUSIC

Lesley and I went to Woodstock. We were living in New York City then. The year was 1969, four years before Burton Lines. We had an apartment at 87th and First. The van was new then, at least new in the used sense. Everything happens to me exactly opposite from how it happens to everyone else.

Woodstock was not fun. I was freaked out by the long-haired hippies, the dope-smoking, and the medical tent for people who were having bad trips on LSD. I had never seen this kind of thing. I wasn't sure what any of it meant or why it was going on. Night one, no acts came on until past midnight, though the bands were supposed to start at noon. It was raining. The heavens had opened. The field we were sitting in, the grassy amphitheater slope on Yasgur's farm, became a sea of mud and refuse.

I had been in San Diego a few years earlier when I got my draft notice, forwarded to General Delivery from my parents' address in New York. The date was September 1965. The Vietnam War was just getting serious. My draft board was in New Rochelle. I hitchhiked back across the country. Three hippies picked me up just outside of Needles on the California-Arizona border. They were returning to their college in Boston after a summer in Haight-Ashbury in San Francisco. All three had long hair and beards. I rode with them for two days, along Route 66 to Oklahoma City. They had come out west, they told me, to take LSD. My first thought was, *Why?* The freaks were ecstatic about what they had experienced. They talked about all the "heads" in "the Haight." LSD was legal then. You went to a concert at the Straight Theater, the freaks told me, and with your ticket you were handed a tab of acid. I couldn't understand it.

Now, at Woodstock, it was clear that something epochal was happening. The youth culture, or whatever you called it, had been thought of by the general public—and by the hippies themselves—as just a few longhairs scattered in odd enclaves from Vermont to San Francisco. But three hundred thousand were gathered here now with more rolling in every minute.

This was a scene.

The world was changing.

Three times in the previous year, my Marine Corps reserve unit had received call-up orders. All were false alarms. We didn't talk about it, my friends in the unit and me. We were weekend warriors, guys who worked on Wall Street or Madison Avenue or had driveway paving businesses in Pelham or Pocantico Hills. We were infantry. For Marines, a tour in Vietnam was thirteen months. Army was twelve. We would come back as hamburger if we came back at all.

I peered around Woodstock at the freaks grooving on Country Joe and the Fish onstage.

And it's one, two, three,
What are we fightin' for?
Don't ask me, I don't give a damn,
Next stop is Vietnam.
And it's five, six, seven,
Open up the Pearly Gates!
Well, ain't no time to wonder why,
Whoopee, we're all gonna die!

Lesley was feeling it too. Given a choice, she and I might not have elected to be part of our generation and have to deal with the issues that confronted it. But, like it or not, we were.

19. BROTHERS

I had two friends from Parris Island and infantry training, brothers from West Virginia named Charles and David McQuade. Charles had an MBA in Finance. He worked as a securities analyst for Equitable Life in Manhattan. He had joined the reserves for the same reason I did—so he wouldn't get drafted into the army. David was five years younger. He had come to New York without a job. He was staying with his brother. He joined just to be with Charles.

Now in New York and finished with our active service, Charles started hanging out with artistic types. They rode motorcycles and grew beards. I had no idea what they were doing. I only saw Charles once a month when we reported to the Naval Reserve Center, but every time his hair was less Leatherneck-like and his eyes had started acquiring a different look. David followed his older brother.

One day Charles called to say he had quit his job. He was moving to San Francisco. This was no small thing. Charles sold everything, down to his Brooks Brothers suits and his Florsheim wingtips. He even got rid of his motorcycle. Lesley and I saw him and David off the night they left. They were taking a driveaway car like Barry Newman in *Vanishing Point*.

"What," I asked Charles, "are you gonna do about the Marine Corps?"

You couldn't just bail. The Department of the Navy would come after you. They'd stick a rifle in your hand and pack you straight out into the shit.

"Fuck the Marine Corps," said Charles.

He had crossed some kind of Rubicon.

Lesley and I looked on in amazement.

Charles sent postcards from San Francisco. He and David had found a place on Twin Peaks. They were taking drugs with names I had never heard of. They seemed to have found something.

Around this time I blew up the book I had been working on, the one I had quit my job eighteen months earlier to write.

The short version is Lesley and I packed the van and went out west too. We were desperate. Maybe a change of coasts would save our marriage.

I had to fill out transfer papers before the Marine Corps would let me make the move. I was assigned to an infantry unit in San Bruno, south of San Francisco. I reported the first day we got to the West Coast. The sergeant checking me in was named Tomasky. "Enjoy the next four weeks," he told me.

"We're getting called up," Tomasky said. He had seen the orders from the Department of the Navy. "Make the most of your last month, buddy. The only way you and me are coming home is as body parts."

Lesley and I found an apartment for seventy dollars a month in a part of San Francisco called "the Avenues." We were out at the very end of the Western world, on a hill overlooking the beach. I got work for a moving company for a dollar-fifty an hour. The thoroughfare along the Pacific was called the Great Highway. There was a club a few blocks down the hill called the Family Dog. The bands that played live were Jefferson Airplane, the Grateful Dead, and It's a Beautiful Day. I had never heard of any of them. But Lesley and I went just because it was so close and the hippies at the door let you in for free. People were more stoned in the Family Dog than they were at Woodstock. Lesley and I were still shocked to witness it.

20. BREAKING UP

Lesley and I split up in San Francisco. She got the apartment and everything we owned. I got the van. I had sixty dollars. She had about the same.

Shame.

I was too ashamed of myself, of being a bad husband, a failure as a provider, of bailing out on my would-be novel after almost two years of being supported by my loving wife, that I could no longer stand her seeing me the way I was.

Where to go?

I decided on New Orleans, partly because I had never been there and neither had anybody I knew. And partly because it seemed to be a place that hadn't yet been rendered plastic by American commercial culture.

The van ticked over one hundred thousand miles somewhere east of Van Horn, Texas. Why did I notice? Why do I still remember? I have no idea. It's not like the miles meant anything.

I had to change reserve units again after moving to Louisiana. The new unit was on Lake Pontchartrain, right on the water. It was the best unit I was ever in, mainly because I never had to attend meetings or go to the field. I reported late one afternoon in January. The NCO in charge was named Mike Bishop. He was a regular Marine, not a reservist—a salty old Gunnery Sergeant, E-6. He had a pile of orders and administration papers on his desk that were clearly driving him crazy.

I said, "I can type."

"Don't shit me."

I volunteered to stay all night.

Gunny Bishop made me a deal. Two nights a month I would come out to the lake. The Gunny would have a pile of typing for me. He'd lock the building with me in it and come back in the morning bringing coffee with chicory and beignets from the Café du Monde. I could sleep on the rack in his office. He gave me the key to the soda machine. I could take any "geedunk" or "pogey bait," i.e., candy, from the vending machine next to it.

"What kinda work you do?"

I shrugged.

"You can always get on in the oil patch," Gunny Bishop said. "Head downriver to Port Sulphur. If you don't find anything there, keep going till you do. There's plenty of work if you don't mind getting dirty."

I thanked the Gunny. We shook hands.

"Keep your hair short and don't do no drugs I wouldn't do."

21. TINSLEY OILFIELD MAINTENANCE

Twenty-five miles downriver from New Orleans is the town of Buras. It's in Plaquemines Parish—parish being the Louisiana term for county. PLACK-uh-mins. You drive past Poydras and Belle Chasse and then go another eight or ten miles to Port Sulphur. Buras is ten more past that. It's oil country. You can catch glimpses of offshore rigs out in the Gulf, but thousands of wells also sit inshore, among the tidal grasslands on both sides of the single two-lane.

At a gas station a kid gave me directions to a place called Tinsley Oilfield Maintenance. "There's no sign," he said. "Look for the glycol tanks on the right, just past the Dixie Mart. Turn into the lot. You'll see a white '58 Ford pickup with a headache rack. That's Tinsley. He'll put you on."

You had to fill out an application to work at Tinsley's. In the middle of the page in double-bold type it said

I AM NOT A HOMOSEXUAL

and

I AM NOT NOW AND HAVE NEVER BEEN A
MEMBER OF THE FASCIST OR COMMUNIST PARTY.

I checked both boxes and signed my name.

"You'll need you a pair of steel-toed boots and a hard hat," said Mrs. Tinsley. She gave me the name of a store in Belle Chasse. "Get you some supper while you're back there. Ain't nothing round here." She indicated two corrugated-tin-sided structures on skids across the shell-paved lot. "Bunkhouses is over there. Pick you a rack now and leave your stuff. Might be a bunch of boys coming in around midnight."

I stayed nine weeks. The last four were offshore. Pay doubled on the rigs to four dollars an hour but the best part was meals were free (steak for dinner every night with unlimited milk from the machine) and every week was eighty hours with forty of that counting as time-and-a-half.

What was going through my mind during this time? Nothing. Blue smoke was pouring out of the van's exhaust. My tires were shot. I couldn't think beyond that. I was utterly miserable with no plan and not even the thought of hope. I didn't think about the past. I had no concept of a future. I was happy to be working, though. I was happy to have a bunk and a place to stay. Things could be a lot worse. The first paycheck came after two weeks. I actually opened an account at a rolling branch of the Mississippi River Bank.

I say "rolling" because everything in Plaquemines Parish at that time was on wheels, even the phone booths, which squatted in pods of three on rigs parked along the roadside. Hurricane Camille had flattened everything in the parish a year earlier. Hundred-foot water towers lay crashed onto their sides in the tidal grass with their steel legs crumpled under them. Churches and schoolhouses were leveled to their foundations. Whole towns had been washed away.

Foremen on crews in this part of Louisiana are called "pushers." Mine was a former Marine named Otis Crowley. These are all real names, by the way.

A trained monkey could do the work we did, offshore or on. Otis showed us everything. "Replace that O ring. Here, lemme show you." "Fetch me a Z12 gasket. Here, lemme show you." Offshore almost every job entailed climbing some rickety superstructure eighty feet above the surface of the Gulf. I liked it.

For inshore work, the crew would be me, Otis, and a seventeen-year-old launch driver named Amory. Launches were fast, inboard-engine cabin vessels. The fields were tidal grasslands that extended for dozens of miles with the savanna-type grass so high you couldn't see over it. Channels ran through the grasslands like roads. How Amory navigated, I have no idea. But he never got us lost.

Wells were spotted everywhere across the dead-flat tidal savanna. Our job was to maintain them. These wells are not like in the movies with tall derricks and James Dean in a cowboy hat striking a gusher; they're just well-heads on platforms the size of a Buick, set two or three feet above the surface of the gulf. Lunch, after what you brought in a paper sack, is supplemented by oysters–called "ersters" in the local vernacular. The tidelands are so shallow you can step off a platform and hit bottom before the water reaches your thighs. Feel down with your fingers and you'll find an oyster. You learn to prize the shells open with a jackknife and suck the juicy, salt and petroleum innards down raw.

The other work you do as a roustabout is in pipe yards. Oilfields need pipe. It's our job—always at night, under the lamps—to load the trucks that haul pipe up and down the inshore compounds. Pipe is loaded with a crane. Your role as a roustabout is to guide the dangling, swinging steel into place on the flatbeds. If your aim is to get your back broken or your skull caved in, this is the job for you. All I remember is staring longingly at the truck drivers, wishing I had their job.

Turns out there was at least one homosexual gentleman in the area. I never saw or met him but, as Otis explained, he had the locals' respect because he was a great bar fighter. "I tell you what," our pusher declared. "That ol' boy may suck a peter, but he sure can kick some ass."

Two good things happened while I was in Plaquemines Parish. One, I began to understand country music. At night my bunkhouse mates and I would sit on the steps, smoking Marlboros and talking. Few were locals. Most were what Otis would call "broke-dick" drifters, casualties of alcohol, divorce, or jail. Without exception they were good guys, who would lend you two bucks when they only had four or pass you their last smoke without a moment's hesitation.

Country songs were about them—their loneliness, their heartbreak, their troubles. Now they were about me too. I had never heard of Eddy Arnold. Now I had to turn my face away when "Then You Can Tell Me Goodbye" came on.

The other good thing was I got Louisiana license plates. I unscrewed my New York plates and threw them into the weeds past the glycol tanks as fast and as far as I could.

LOUISIANA

with an illustration of a pelican and

SPORTSMAN'S PARADISE.

It's impossible to overstate what a difference those plates made in how people responded to me.

22. SPORTSMAN'S PARADISE

I just want to be a regular guy. I want the crazy shit in my head to stop. I want to have a job, just a simple job that a regular guy can do, with a place to stay, maybe meet a nice girl someday. How did I get to be this person I am, who can't do anything, who lives in fear twenty-four hours a day, possesses no skills and no sense of what he wants or how, even if he did know, he could get there?

I began obsessing about Lesley. To phone her was beyond my emotional capacity. I wrote her a postcard. Thank God I don't have that card today. I can't imagine what I put on paper. She wrote back. She had met a guy. She was living with him.

I could feel myself going down a very dark hole. Somehow the idea formed that I had to get back to Lesley. I had to win her back. This seemed to make sense, listening to the lyrics of country songs. My rear axle bearing was failing. My radiator core had holes in it wide enough to stick a wrench-handle into. All four tires were slicks. I had four hundred bucks with another one-twenty coming in two checks. I put three-forty into repairs, left a forwarding address with Tinsley for the checks, and took off.

My last stop was with Gunny Bishop at the reserve center on Lake Pontchartrain. He put in my transfer papers back to San Bruno. I typed them and mimeographed them. The Gunny let me work four days for credit so I wouldn't have to report to San Bruno for another couple of months.

I just want to be a regular guy.

For some reason the fiasco with the dropped trailer has not counted against me. If anything, it has cemented my position on the drivers' roster. "You've got a big-ass fuck-up on your charge sheet now," Byron tells me. "That puts you in the club."

Hugh Reaves sends me to Bradenton, Florida, with Harold, to Bermuda Hundred in Petersburg, Virginia, with Sammy, and to Ronceverte, West Virginia, with Byron. "Watch how Byron handles those downhills. You're gonna have to drive 'em yourself one of these days and I don't want to be sending no one to scrape your ass off the side of a mountain."

Mountains in the South are not like the Rockies out west. You're not climbing Rabbit Ears Pass at nine thousand feet. But the Virginia/West Virginia mountains have something that the Rockies don't—fierce ups and downs and rights and lefts.

Ronceverte is the town right next to White Sulphur Springs, where the Greenbrier resort is. The load is paper for cigarette packs in two sixteen-thousand-pound industrial rolls in a high-cube trailer. The shipment must be delivered at 0630 when the warehouse opens. That means driving the twisting, unlit two-lane across eighty-plus miles of up-and-down Virginia hills between three and six in the morning, when the ridge mist fills the tunnel-like canopy between the elms and hickories and when fierce downhills push the speedometer needle to eighty and beyond. Byron, of course, handles the roller-coaster landscape like it's nothing. I'm hanging on for dear life.

Byron shifts like Harold and Sammy, without the clutch. "Harold show you 'bout taking the slack out?" Byron flicks on the dome light and has me watch the throw between gears. "When you come out of one gear into neutral, don't hang around in the middle. Push against the next gear. Gently. You'll feel the teeth resist you. Don't rush. Wait for the RPMs to synch. When she's ready, she'll open up and let you in."

The cabin of Byron's 324-T is as spare as a space capsule. The deck is steel, like the dash, without an item of driver-comfort anywhere—exactly the way a truck should be. Beneath your soles are the heavy-duty clutch (untouched), the flat-press brake pedal, steel with grooves, and the throttle beside it, worn and shiny with wear. The parking brake with its pull-knob pressure release and air pressure gauge take up the extreme left of the facing. The instrument panel itself is fourteen round dials in two rows flanking the steering column—air pressure, oil pressure, coolant temperature, speed, RPMs, oil temperature, fuel gauge, battery capacity, and so on.

The trailer brake is on the column, a slender stalk just beneath the spokes of the steering wheel. No A/C. Crank-down windows. No power accessories anywhere. A fan the size of your hand sits on the far-right of the dash. The heater is feebler than the one in a VW bus. The engine is beneath and behind you. You feel and hear the diesel growl coming up through your soles and the seat of your pants. The only item of comfort in the cab is the driver's seat, which elevates and absorbs shock pneumatically and is built solid as the pilot's seat in a fighter plane. The shift lever is stout steel, twenty-four inches long, mounted on the deck and ascending to the right side of the driver's seat. Its worn knob seats itself perfectly into the palm of your right hand.

"Only one way to drive these mountains and that's with balls of brass." Byron says this as 324-T plunges like the lead car on a roller coaster down a pitch-black, twisting, blind-corner two-lane with no sign or indication of when the downhill ends and a life-preserving uphill heaves into view. I peer toward Byron's speedometer. The needle is buried against the right-hand pin. "We're gonna need every bit of that speed," Byron says, "when we hit the next uphill."

My eyeballs are the size of saucers, squinting ahead. When the grade appears, Byron hits it like a freight train. Just like he says, the uphill absorbs all the momentum in seconds. Byron shows me how to skip gears downshifting. Tenth to seventh to fourth and even lower.

Byron teaches me how to slow the truck on these crazy down-plunges. "Transmission's everything on these sonsofbitches. But you can't let her get away from you. That load behind us is thirty-six thousand pounds with another twenty-six thousand in the cab. When that shit starts pushing the truck on these five-mile downhills, you can't hold her with your main brakes. Y'ever see brakes afire? Use your trailer brake. Just touch 'er. Don't do no more'n a tap on your main brakes. You know what a jack-knife is. It takes two men and a boy to turn the wheel once you're in one."

We've come out of the uphill and into another roller-coaster plummet.

"Stay in gear. Use the transmission. That's all you got on these steep motherfuckers. Don't never, never come out of gear."

As he says this, 324-T's speedometer reads eighty-one and climbing, with the narrow lightless two-lane plunging like the Cyclone at Coney Island and twisting wildly left into the darkness.

"Sit chilly," chants Byron. He says it as much to himself as to me.

24. MILK, POWDERED (USDA#1)

One of the contracts Burton Lines has with the State of North Carolina is to deliver surplus food to needy communities along the coast. For the driver, this is the lowest-paying load on the docket. Eleven dollars out and back. Sammy Hunt sets a hand on my shoulder. "These sonsofbitches," he says, "has got your name all over 'em."

I don't mind. From the first, these trips become my favorites.

The surplus food comes in cardboard boxes that are loaded by hand by prisoners, all young, all black, at a warehouse on Gate 2 Road in Butner, ten miles northeast of Durham.

MILK, POWDERED (USDA #1)

BEANS, PINTO (CANNED)

CHEESE, BLOCK (USDA #2)

This is bulk food; the cartons are big and heavy. Cheese in twenty-pound slabs. Beans in twenty-four can cases. Dried beans in twenty-pound bags, rice in fifty-pound sacks. The guards won't let you talk to the prisoners as they wheel their hand trucks up from the belly of the warehouse and shuttle in and out of the trailer. But nobody stops you from slipping a guy a couple of Marlboros or a Nehi Grape.

The government food is delivered to and distributed by churches. The minister is the man authorized to sign the manifest. I never saw one that wasn't black.

The load is always delivered first thing, meaning six in the morning.

But from the warehouse to the coast is three or four hours tops. Communities out there are so rural they're barely on the map. Grantsboro, Currituck, Aurora; Plymouth, Roper, Merry Hill. Because the drive is so short, you don't have to leave till two or three in the morning.

I take my time and enjoy the night.

Traffic is nonexistent at that hour once you get onto the secondary roads. I aim to get to the church an hour before delivery. The lots, invariably unpaved, are empty then. You can pick a spot and back in without worrying about cars coming and going. I'll snooze in the sleeper berth or just walk around and take in the morning.

Few settings in the world are as charming as these unremarked coastal towns, particularly in summer, and particularly in the cool just as the sun is peeking forth. The land is flat this close to the coast. It's "low country." Tidal bays and inlets extend across vistas two and three miles broad. On a night with a moon, you'll see a causeway or an elevated bridge reflecting in the distance. The ground beneath your boots is sandy. Spiny oak leaves and sawgrass fronds crunch under your soles. The smell is musty and fecund. Spanish moss hangs from the elbows of the live oaks. Signs are hand-painted out here. Almost always they're misspelled.

The protocol around these deliveries is as strict as it is unspoken. The minister always addresses you as "driver." No one asks your name or speaks to you by any moniker other than your occupation.

"Driver, would you pull your vehicle forward a few feet please? So the recipients can enter and park yonder."

The manifest is scrutinized line by line and left unsigned by the receiving party until its categories and figures have been determined to match the trailer's actual contents. This individual is often not the minister but an allied personage, presumably a member of the congregation, whose title or position possesses some official standing with the state of North Carolina.

Breaking the seal on the trailer is always witnessed, often by the minister reinforced by a congregation elder, usually female, and always in the most scrupulous manner.

"Thank you, driver. We'll take it from here."

The minister will not let you assist with the off-loading. He has congregation members, or the food recipients themselves, for that. The assigned parishioners have climbed aboard. They're physically in the trailer, among the rows of boxes. They pass the stuff out, one case or carton at a time, over the rear deck.

The recipients arrive in ones and twos—in pickups and sedans, field cars and farm tractors towing harvesting wagons or flats, as well as the odd horse- or mule-drawn cart, rail- or stake-sided, often with auto tires. They come early, in the pre-dawn cool. I station myself to the side somewhere, so I can keep an eye on the truck, which is after all my responsibility, but also so as not to embarrass the recipients.

In truth I feel privileged to have a window onto this world. I'm shy about it. I don't want to intrude. In thirty or forty trips over a year or more, I said barely a word to one of the recipients. A nod or a smile, that's it. And nobody said a word to me.

Winter trips possess their own frigid flavor. I get to the terminal at one or two in the morning. The yard is deserted. Half-frozen condensation clings to the steel door of the utility compartment as I open it. The compartment is at eye height, above and to the rear of the step-up to the cab.

Inside are my boots and coveralls, tool kit and first aid box, gloves and rain gear and heavy rubber bungee cords. I reach past the pile of paperbacks I'm reading to the aerosol dispenser of Valvoline starting fluid. I pull it out and give the can a good shake.

Truck engines start hard in the cold. A diesel has no spark plugs. The fuel combusts in the cylinders by compression alone. Sometimes this process needs help. Starter fluid is a mixture of diethyl ether and heptane. I have no idea what either of them are but they fire up fast. I clamber over the saddle tank onto the truck's frame and crabwalk under the cab from beneath and behind. It's like burrowing into the crawlspace under a house. I'm crouched on the frame with the engine block six inches from my nose. A hinged cover sits on the air intake. I lift it, turn the can of starter fluid upside-down and give her a quick shot.

I scoot back up into the cab and press the starter. Gotta move fast before the fluid evaporates. The diesel growls to life. It's a great sound. The smell is even better. Why is this shit so important to me? I don't know. But to fire up a truck is an orgasmic experience. It feels great to know how to do it and to see that it works.

I climb down from the cab, replace the starter fluid in its corner of the utility compartment, shut the door, and secure it tightly.

You can't simply start up a tractor-trailer and pull out onto the highway. Trucks have air brakes. The compressor has to charge the tanks up to the required pressure before the brakes will release. When you set the parking brake on a truck, the system switches from air-driven to spring-loaded. The reason it does this is because air tanks will bleed out over minutes or hours. If you were to stop on the road for a piece of pie and a coffee, you could come back out and find you've got nothing. That's why the parking brakes are spring-loaded. Conversely, when you're starting up, the spring-loaded brakes won't release until the pressure builds to the proper threshold for the air brakes to take over.

So I let the engine idle while I do my full by-the-book walkaround—crab-walking under the trailer to check the angle and slack of the brake arms, bleed the moisture from the air tanks, peer up behind the "fifth wheel" to make sure the kingpin is securely yoked; then scrambling out, I check fuel, oil, water, and battery. Back up into the cab to check the headlights on high and low beams, parking lights, clearance lights, brake lights, four-way flashers, and turn signals on both tractor and trailer. The engine is warm now; air pressure is up so the parking brake will release. I tug down on the hand valve on the side of the steering column to set the trailer brakes, depress the clutch, shift into first and ease off gently. The free tractor strains against the locked wheels of the trailer. Now I know I'm coupled good and solid. I line up the mirrors, check the wipers and defroster, wheel horn and air horn, emergency switch, and axle interlock.

I climb down again from the cab, easing out backward and hanging onto the handgrips, looking down between my legs as I step from fender to footplate to the dirt of the yard. I clamber up over the saddle tanks to the frame immediately behind the tractor, check the "handshaker" clasps on the air brake lines to the trailer, inspect the electrical cable and plug, then scoot down again to do a final walkaround, checking all eighteen tires and finally the load lock and seal on the trailer. Tonight I'm pulling a box trailer so I don't have to worry about tie-downs,

Back in the cab, I fill out my logbook. Can't tell you how much I enjoy this. Name, vehicle ID number, home terminal, date. There's a twenty-four-hour graphic, like a radio dial running left to right across the page. It starts at midnight on the left and runs to midnight on the right. Four sections:

OFF DUTY

SLEEPER BERTH

DRIVING

ON DUTY

The DOT only allows you so many hours in twenty-four where you're either on duty or driving. It's like being an airline pilot. The feds don't want you nodding off behind the wheel.

I tug the stubby pencil from its slot in the logbook cover. I trace a horizontal line starting in OFF DUTY, dropping down to ON DUTY for half an hour, then up to DRIVING. I fill in the blanks for shipping document number, commodity, FROM, TO, etc. I press hard so the carbon copies take and then close the cover before I toss the book into the green steel incline atop the dash.

Check the map, memorize the route.

Air pressure is fully up now. Pull-release the knob on the left of and below the instrument panel. That's the hiss you hear.

The one time you use the clutch, other than shutting down, is to shift into first. Check the mirrors one last time, check instrument illumination, depress the accelerator.

We're on the move.

25. LIGHTS OUT

April 27. I'm taking two eighteen-thousand-pound rolls of printed cigarette-pack paper from Spotswood, New Jersey, to Spartanburg, South Carolina, at night in the rain when I glance in the left outboard mirror and see that my lights are out. The whole trailer is dark. Fuck!

No way to keep driving. The first cop will stop me and write me up. For sure I'll lose my job, which is hanging by a thread already.

I find a turnout and pull over. This is on SC 29 about ten miles east of Gaffney. Two-lane blacktop, unlit. Loblolly pines on both sides. The rain is intensifying. I've phoned for help so many times. I can't call Hugh Reaves again. Besides, it's two in the morning. He's home asleep.

I climb down from the cab and haul myself up over the left-hand saddle tank onto the frame between the tractor and the trailer. It's Spring and cold. All I've got is a jean jacket. I'm soaked already.

Electrical power for the trailer comes from the cab. A heavy insulated line extends on coil suspenders to a receptacle on the front face of the trailer. The trailer has four sets of mandated illumination—running lights, clearance lights, backup lights, and brake lights. I find the plug and inspect it. Somehow the unit has been wrenched free and fallen between the saddle tanks. It has dragged on the road. The plug is mangled; wires sprout like loose spaghetti—red, yellow, blue, green, black. I have no idea which wire goes to which connector or even if power will be restored if I succeed in reconnecting them. No one taught us this at the school. Nor have Harold and Sammy and Byron included such instruction in my on-the-job curriculum.

Short version: two hours later I'm soaked to the skin and crying. I mean sobbing. Shoulders shaking, tears sheeting down my cheeks.

Why am I like this?

What is wrong with me?

I can't figure this fucking plug out.

But I have to. I have a load to deliver. I can't call Hugh Reaves again. I have to solve this goddam thing.

I'm excruciatingly aware of my emotional state and how ineffective and shameful it is. Harold would have no problem with this. Sammy or Ernie or Charley Stewart would see it simply as a problem to be solved. They would bring no emotion to the situation. They'd focus and fix it.

I have come utterly unpeeled. I can't stop crying. My hands are shaking. Four in the morning and I'm no closer to solving this puzzle than I was when I started.

I realize, with further burning self-reproach, that my state of mind is no accident. This is how I handle emergencies. I make myself helpless so that some Other Force or Person, seeing my plight, will take pity and help. Who?

I'm so wet and cold I can't think.

I climb down off the frame, haul myself back into the cab and try to summon poise and rationality. A writing implement, that's what I need. I find my stubby pencil and a scrap of paper—a page torn from my logbook—dismount again from the cab and work back to my perch on the frame. I've got my mini-flashlight clamped between my teeth, trying to shine it onto the paper.

YELLOW WIRE (I draw an arrow to) TOP HOLE ON PLUG.

Every one of the five color-coded wires has to be re-inserted and screwed down in its proper receptor in the plug. I have no reference to draw upon. No indicator. No instruction.

I try them one by one. Each combination. Each permutation.

Nothing.

No lights.

The truck is idling so I have power.

Another half-hour passes. My watch says 3:55. I must have tried fifty combinations. Then:

Somehow the clearance lights come on.

Do I dare drive with just these? Without brake lights?

Fuck!

BLUE ... LEFT FROM TOP
BLACK ... FIRST RIGHT
RED ... SECOND RIGHT

I try each color wire in each hole, one by one, in every conceivable combination.

To test if the brake lights are working, I have to climb back into the cab, press the brake pedal and watch in the mirrors for the lights' reflection on the ground.

For backup lights, shift into reverse, watch for red on the dirt.

Forty minutes later I've got it.

Somehow.

No clue how.

I seal the plug as best I can and reseat it into the receptacle.

It's working.

I have running lights, clearance lights, brake lights, backup lights.

Of course, now it's almost daylight so I don't need them.

I climb back into the cab and drive on.

I deliver the load.

This is, without a doubt, the hardest thing I've ever done in my life.

I'm soaked through. My hands are blue. My knuckle joints have entered rigor mortis.

At Spartanburg that morning, the dock supervisor tells me he's got a load of wire wheels going to Spanish Fort, Florida. He has phoned Hugh Reaves and I'm to take it on. After that I deadhead to Burton's satellite terminal in Waycross, Georgia, drop my Hi-Cube trailer and pick up a flatbed. From there I'm to drive back to North Carolina, to the port of Wilmington, to pick up a load of steel plates and take it to Hopewell, Virginia. Then to the Richmond Guano Company for bagged fertilizer destined for the Archer Bros. feed and grain store in Scotland Neck, North Carolina.

Four days later I'm pulling back into the yard at Durham.

"How'd it go?" asks Hugh Reaves.

"Great," I say. "No problems."

Twenty-two years later, in Hollywood, I'm working on a rewrite for Frank Price and Jack Epps at MGM. The project is called *Mister X*. The text we're working from is *The Return of Mister X*, a graphic novel by Bert, Mario & Jaime Hernandez and Dean Motter.

I have fallen in love with Mister X. He's me. He's everyone. He's contemporary man boiled down to his excruciating essentials.

Mister X is a creature of the urban night. His garb is a black ankle-length duster with the collar turned up. His skull is shaved. His skin is pale. Stubble pocks his cheeks. Mister X wears round, bug-eye protective goggles; even the pallid glare of the nocturnal city is painful to his eyes.

Mister X has no special powers except his own hyperbolic sensitivity and paranoia. He can feel a lost lady's loneliness at a range of half a block. His nervous system is attuned to the woes of the Gotham-like/German Expressionist metropolis called Radiant City whose avenues and alleys he designed years ago and which he now haunts. His soul shudders with the collective anguish, heartbreak, and despair of the city.

Mister X has a nemesis. His name is Zamora. I work on the script for four months and I never figure out exactly who Zamora is, except that he's a bad, bad man and he wants Mister X dead.

Mister X has girlfriends, three of them—Patrice, who calls him Michael; Mercedes, who addresses him as Santos; and the passionate exotic Consuelo, for whom he is Walter. No one of Mister X's lovers knows any of the others, yet each is keenly and painfully aware that she has competition. Each knows Mister X as a completely different individual. And Mister X himself is a different person with each of his paramours.

In other words, it's exactly like real life.

I want desperately to make the next draft of the screenplay work. I want to supply that stroke of revision genius that puts this story over the top and makes the studio say, "Yes, we will put it into production." Why? Because I want to see this movie. I want to see it cast. I want to see it shot. I want to see what a great director and cinematographer and production designer (not to mention actors and actresses) can do to bring this vision to celluloid life. Mister X is not some bogus superhero like Batman or Superman. His anguish is yours and mine. It's everyone's.

But Jack and Frank and I can't make it work and neither can the previous writers and subsequent writers. Our combined exertions leave *Mister X* short of consummation. Please forgive us, Hernandez brothers and Dean Motter.

Sometimes, as hard as you try, you just can't do it.

27. SIMPKINSVILLE, PART TWO

Bruce's mechanic shop in Simpkinsville has no indoor warming elements except a single kerosene heater beside the front roll-up doors. I'm hovering there. Bruce himself climbs up from the below-ground pit, having finished his examination of my poor van. He says he can do an engine rebuild—the job will take about a week—for four hundred bucks. "But I can't lend you my Ford like we talked about, sorry."

Bruce tells me he sold the pickup to Lesley, just three days ago. "She come by with her mother and two hundred dollars in twenties."

We cross the T-intersection to his cousin Hattie's country store and drink hot coffee by the wood-burning stove. Bruce tells me Lesley has graduated from the same truck driving school in Raleigh that I went to. She already has a job with UPS, driving sets of doubles between their terminals at Raleigh and Greensboro and Winston-Salem. "Starts in a couple days, I think. Union job, with medical and everything."

Bruce peers around the yard, seeking a vehicle he can lend me while mine is in the shop. I tell him not to worry. If he can give me a ride home, or get someone around the shop to, I can work out transportation with friends at work or just stay on the road till the rebuild can be finished.

"How you doin' over there?" Bruce knows the family story. He probably understands the deep dynamics better than I do. He urges me to come back to the fellowship. I promise to try.

"I've got nine hundred bucks in the Wachovia bank," I tell him. "A house my landlady rents has come open. I'm gonna take it, get out of where I am."

Bruce has a pegboard in his tiny office at the corner of the shop. He hangs my keys on the second lug, meaning my rebuild comes up as soon as he finishes the job he's working on now. He drives me back to the Burton terminal, where I've got a load waiting for Reidsville and another from there to Ronceverte, West Virginia. We shake hands just as the leading edge of an Atlantic storm moves in. "Think about the fellowship," he says.

28. BURYING THE NEEDLE

The stretch over the mountains is sixty-two miles from Roanoke, a good-sized town in the Virginia foothills, to Ronceverte/White Sulphur Springs in West Virginia. It's night and coal-dark. The passage starts with a long uphill pull to the town of Newcastle. Your nerves are tightening the whole way, knowing every foot of elevation you're gaining now must be paid for with twisting, screaming downhills in the final twenty to thirty miles. This is Potts Mountain Road. No lights. Few if any curve-indication signs. The only yellow reflectors you see are those snaky, zig-zag arrows.

TRUCKERS MAX SAFE SPEED NEXT 5 MILES 25 MPH

The first issue is curves. Some you can take at forty. In others, fifteen is too hot. And you don't know when these curves are coming or how long they'll go on once you're in them. The road is so narrow you hear tree branches scraping the flanks of your trailer. The two-lane is like a tunnel. No sky above, nothing but darkness right or left. You hit a flat and think you can breathe, then out of nowhere your right front tires graze a white picket fence. Your headlights show a dog on a chain. You're half into somebody's front yard.

A sign says Peters Mountain. My ears are popping. Potts Mountain. Turtle Creek. Sweet Chalybeate. The road is diving and ascending. I'm chanting Byron's mantra, "Sit chilly," and trying to release my death grip on the wheel and the shift lever.

When a sixty-eight-thousand-pound vehicle approaches a severe uphill, it needs to be carrying all the speed it possibly can. If you could strike an uphill at a hundred miles an hour, you would do it because the rising grade slows you down so fast you wind up downshifting furiously and potentially dangerously as your speed drops—tenth to ninth to eighth to skip-a-gear to skip-two-gears—because if you miss a shift you can wind up without power while your speed is dropping so fast you don't know what gear to jump into next.

At the same time going downhill in these mountains, the weight of your vehicle is making you plummet like an anvil dropped off a skyscraper. Using a lower gear helps only so much. The plunge is too steep. You tap the tractor brakes and downshift fast in the interval when the truck slows and downshift again if you dare. It's ten times scarier than an uphill because if you miss a shift here, you're freewheeling and there's no coming back. Do you dare touch the brakes again? Yeah, on a stretch that's straight. But swooping and sweeping around wild corners? You can feel the rear eight wheels grab. But now your ten wheels up front are literally elevating off the road, not to mention if you're in a curve on slick asphalt your ass-end is starting to fishtail.

A downhill in these mountains might be a quarter mile long, which would be good. Or it might be four miles. The problem is you don't know. You haven't driven the road enough times to have memorized its hazards. And because you don't know the road, you don't know if the downhill you're on that's driving your speedometer to sixty, sixty-five, seventy, seventy-five turns into an uphill in a quarter mile or a half mile or maybe two miles, at which point if you don't brake or use your transmission now to slow yourself by some means of magic, you'll be doing two hundred and ten. And the road keeps turning so you can't see ahead. A long left. Where's the bottom? Is that it ahead? Now we're reeling to the right. Eighty per. Eighty-five. Where's the bottom? You're going so fast that even if the road stays clear, with no oncoming headlights blinding you, you still can't stay on it. You're simply moving too fast.

But what makes the ordeal even more terrifying are the drivers from Smith's Transfer. Smith's Transfer is a big interstate freight company based in Staunton, Virginia. Staunton is in the mountains. Smith's drivers make these runs every night. What does that mean? It means these cowboys know the road. They know when a right turn is coming or a left. They know when a downhill is eight hundred yards long and not fourteen hundred. This means they can bury the needle. They know when to back off and when to let their speed run away with them.

Are these Smith's Transfer boys sane, responsible operators? Fuck no. They are wild-ass mountain men whose heroes are Junior Johnson and Richard Petty. Me, I'm just trying to survive and deliver a load. I hear an air horn behind me and see high-beams flash in my mirrors. A Smith's Transfer driver is flush on my ass, blaring at me to get the hell out of his way. The road is two-lane blacktop with no turnouts and no passing lanes. Honk honk. What can I do? I have to go as fast as he's going. But he knows the road. I don't. What's even scarier is glancing in your mirrors and seeing him *not* behind you. That means he knows to slow down because something hairy is coming up ahead.

I finish each mountain crossing wrung to a frazzle. My fondest hope phoning in to Hugh Reaves is to be sent on to Kentucky or Tennessee to pick up another load now that the Green Season has started, and live tobacco is actually being hauled, just so I can loop back home on level ground and in daylight.

"I've got good news," says Hugh this time. "Deadhead home by any route you like. But get here fresh. Mr. Martin is calling a meeting. He wants every driver there and everyone wide awake."

Ed Martin is the only person at Burton Lines who wears a necktie. I've seen him before, conferring with Hugh Reaves in the dispatcher's office or crossing the driver's room on his way back to his office in the administrative half of the building. But I've never actually spoken to him or even been introduced. Is he a manager or VP? Does he own the company?

My name on the appointment sheet is paired with Byron and another black driver named Jesse Conover. It's seven-thirty on a stifling September evening. Ed Martin and his secretary wait for us in his office. She serves coffee in Styrofoam cups and donuts on paper plates. We sit— Byron, Jesse, and me—on folding steel chairs, like for a funeral, across from Mr. Martin's heavy, gunmetal-gray desk.

"Y'all, don't be nervous. The company isn't firing you or cutting your pay."

After a minute or two of chitchat and friendly inquiries about the health and well-being of each individual and his family, Mr. Martin clears his throat and explains that he has called this meeting, and the others with the other drivers, to present each Burton Lines employee with a professional opportunity. He asks that we hear him out. No decision needs to be made tonight or even in the next few weeks. "Go home and think about it. Talk it over with your wives and families."

Individual information packets have been set on our chairs. Jesse Conover thumbs through his fast. I'm trying to assimilate mine.

"Give it to us straight, Mr. Martin," says Byron.

"All right, here it is."

The company, Mr. Martin says, wants to change the way it works with its drivers. "We want to switch from an employee-hire model to an independent-contractor model. The short version is we want each of you to buy your truck—the one you're driving now—and work with Burton Lines as owner-operators instead of employees.

"Look at your information packets. Byron, Jesse, Steve... each one has been put together for you personally, for your individual piece of equipment."

Byron speaks. "Is this same deal being put before Harold and Sammy and everybody?"

"Everybody," says Mr. Martin. "Every driver gets the same opportunity."

The meeting continues for half an hour. The nutshell is Burton has made a deal with Burlington National Bank. For any driver who wishes to, the bank will finance the purchase of the tractor he is driving now. My truck, 306-T, I read, can be acquired for $2,200. Burlington Bank will lend me the money with a payback period of ten years.

The typical month's payment will be $83.

"Interest," says Mr. Martin, "is, of course, tax-deductible."

Burton Lines will maintain the equipment, that is, assume responsibility for all repairs, refits, rebuilds, including tires and service and maintenance for a flat fee of thirty dollars a month. Burton Lines will pay all insurance.

The company will act as freight agent for the drivers. It'll find the work. It'll assign the loads. It will dispatch each driver, with his truck, exactly as it does now. Hugh Reaves will remain our dispatch agent, though no longer our boss and supervisor.

Burton will split with each driver, fifty-fifty, the revenue from all loads delivered.

"You and Burton Lines will be partners," says Mr. Martin. "The only difference is you'll be getting half of the profit from each load you deliver instead of a weekly salary. In other words, the more you work, the more you earn."

The final page of the info pack is an estimate of what each of our take-homes will be under this new system, based upon the previous three months of work we've done under the existing system.

My pay, according to this projection, will more than double.

The meeting ends. Jesse, Byron, and I drive straight to Byron's home on Rovere Road in Durham.

"This is bullshit," Byron declares immediately and empathically. "The company's trying to fuck us in the ass and sugar-coating it so we bend over and take it."

Byron's wife Tita brings coffee and sweet rolls. She clears the kids out of the kitchen. She herself returns, taking the chair beside her husband under the CAMELS MILD lamp. All of us are smoking. The tin ashtray in front of me says DUKE SPORT SHOP. Byron's and Tita's is enamel:

BEVERLY OSBORNE'S "CHICKEN IN THE ROUGH"

"Bet your ass," Byron says, "the company went over the books and found that vehicle maintenance, insurance, and whatever-the-fuck-else is costing them a fortune. They know every swinging dick in that driver's room has got a record. Can't none of us get on nowhere else. So it's shifting all risk and liability onto us."

Jesse speaks. "What scares the shit outa me is my truck. Bitch got 370,000 miles on her. Fourth engine rebuild. What if she goes down again?"

My turn. "Mr. Martin says we don't have to take the deal. We can continue on salary just like now."

"For how long?" says Byron.

A part of me is thinking something I don't dare say. I'm humbled and grateful that the company has included me in this offer. Bogus or not, ill-intentioned or not, it feels great to be on the list with Byron and Harold and Sammy.

The other thing I don't say, for fear of offering offense, is that the company's regular contract loads—tobacco in hogsheads, paper in rolls, steel, fertilizer, and other primarily flatbed freight—are so low on the food chain that no competitor (certainly not Pilot or Akers or Carolina Freight) is going to go after them.

We're safe. Harold said this the first day I met him. No other company wants the loads Burton Lines carries, and no other group of drivers is willing to do the dirty labor we do.

Mr. Martin's offer could be a good deal.

I'm thinking of that house my landlady said had just come available.

I'm thinking of Lesley with her new job at UPS and her union paycheck.

What if I owned my own truck? What if I lived in a decent house? What if I had a freight contract and a steady income going forward?

Could Lesley and I get back together?

Would she be willing, at least, to think about it?

Harold and Sammy have decided to take the company's offer. They're going a step further and throwing in with Ernie Beale from the body shop and a mechanic named Junior from Charley Stewart's crew. Harold and Sammy will finance the purchase of their own trucks; Ernie and Junior will do the same for Jesse Conover and a white driver named Denny, who either can't afford to buy their own trucks or don't want the risk and responsibility.

Harold invites me to come in with them. "With six trucks," he says, "we can form our own corporation. We'll be an outfit. Our own outfit."

As a legitimate business entity, Harold says, we can negotiate a group insurance plan. "Medical, dental, liability. I'm paying through the ass right now for the kids and getting nothing. There's tax advantages to something like this that none of us has even thought about. This is how the smart boys get rich, son, not selling their sweat hour-by-hour like we do."

It's October now. I make an appointment one night and sit down in the office with Hugh Reaves. He stays late, for no reason other than to help me. Cigarette smoke rises from his MANGUM STREET TIRES ashtray. With the terminal lights reflecting from outside and the desk lamp burning from directly above, Mr. Reaves goes through the numbers with me on a yellow legal pad.

I was never a good Marine. I don't dare tell Hugh Reaves what trouble I've gotten into over the years. Crazy as it sounds, though, that's the bond between us. That's why he's sitting with me now. It's why he took a chance on me in the first place.

"I'm thinking about throwing in with Harold and Sammy." I volunteer nothing about Lesley. Hugh Reaves doesn't even know I have a wife, let alone that I haven't seen her or spoken with her in almost a year. I keep my mouth shut about her job with UPS and about my hopes of renting a decent house.

"I just don't want you getting ahead of yourself," the former staff sergeant says as the ashtrays fill and darkness deepens outside. "Six months ago, you were dropping trailers and pissing in your pants going over Potts Mountain."

31. DISTANCE

I don't know Lesley's number so I can't phone. Her mother directs me when I show up unannounced at her farmhouse on a late October Sunday. It's ten in the morning. My wife's new place is on State Road 231 south of Wendell. The road has no actual name. I find it by looking out for Bruce Simpkins' '59 Ford pickup, the one he sold Lesley, parked out front.

With the economy in the toilet, a number of farmhouses in the area have become available for rent. Lesley's sits on a rise about an eighth of a mile off the two-lane with cleared chalky fields in front and pine woods on three sides behind. The house itself is white, or was fifty years ago when it was first painted. Like every other in the area, it hasn't seen a coat since. A broad shaded porch presents its front and side to the rising approach.

I turn up the dirt drive. I can see Lesley out front. She's alone. She spots the van at a distance and straightens. When I get closer, I see she's splitting pine quarters for kindling. A flat stump serves as a chopping block. She stops and sets the axe aside, leaning it, handle-up, against a mound of split pine.

Already I know this visit is a bad idea.

But I'm here. I can't stop now.

The spot where Lesley's standing is on a slight rise. She's above me as I step down from the van and cross toward her. Hi, how are you? What are you doing here? Sorry, I would've phoned first, but...

Lesley is fearing a scene. She's afraid I'm going to say something desperate or pathetic. In my head I'm rehearsing my plan for buying 306-T and getting a house. At once this sounds desperate and pathetic.

I hear my voice congratulating her on finishing the driving school. She finished number two in her class, she says. "Just like you." We talk about Bruce for a minute, and about her mother and sisters. Everyone is fine. I commend her on the house. It's pretty. "The porch is falling down," she says, "and there's not a floor that's level or a door that's plumb. But I'm working on it."

I'm thinking of what Harold said on that trip to Ancram, about the "spell" his first wife had over him and about the moment when he finally realized he was free of it. My experience in this moment is the opposite. I look at Lesley's face, her eyes that turn down at the corners giving her aspect a certain sweet sadness, her long hair shiny the way it blows across her cheeks in the wind.

I'm desperately bound to her. Nothing's changed. If anything, it's worse. The distance between her and me seems measured in light-years. I feel it in my knees. I have to force my soles into the dirt to hold steady.

Lesley is talking about the wood stove she got for twenty dollars from her neighbor down below the pond. As she speaks, the weirdest double reversal occurs. I had driven over with nothing but my own fears and intentions in mind. Now at once all I can feel are hers.

This moment is a horror for her. I'm torturing her, showing up like this. Every sinew, every aspect of her posture and distance is screaming, "Go away! Please just go!"

I want to help her. I'm frantic to end her torment. If I could, I would turn around and run. I would vaporize. But I'm here. I have to face this out.

For Lesley's part, I can see that the nightmare of finding me before her is turned on its head by her care for me. She knows me. She's seen the worst and she's seeing it again now. It must break her heart to see someone she once loved enough to marry, enough to speak the word "forever," now so far gone and grasping so excruciatingly at straws.

I'm asking her about her new job. How's it going? How does she like it?

It's fun, she says. "I take a set of doubles every night from the UPS terminal in Raleigh to the sister terminal in Winston-Salem... some nights Greensboro, other nights Charlotte... and come back with a different set, already loaded when I pull in."

Lesley asks how I'm doing. She has heard via Bruce that I'm looking at a little house in the country out toward Creedmoor. I confirm this. I advance a step up the rise toward her. She backs away. Her eyes scan past me, down the hill toward the two-lane, as if hoping that someone, anyone, will appear and drive up to say hello.

I can't put her through this much longer. I blurt the idea of buying my truck, that maybe she and I could... what?

"Please," she says.

I'm hurting her. I can't keep doing this. I withdraw a step. Lesley's shoulders lower slightly. Her glance keeps darting away down the hill.

I can't speak any more. How can I end this? I feel it in my heart, like a hand crushing everything in the center of my chest.

Lesley is squinting toward the van. I have washed it, down to the wheel rims, before driving over. "Do you remember," she asks, "when you used to pick me up at A.G. Becker on Friday evenings in the summer?"

This is the Wall Street brokerage she worked for as a secretary when we first lived in New York City and I was an office boy at Grey Advertising. We'd head down to North Carolina each Friday, driving all night, to the coast. We'd sleep in the van Saturday night, have breakfast Sunday morning at Topsail Beach, then drive back, five hundred miles, all day Sunday to be in the city for work Monday morning.

"I remember the other secretaries," Lesley says, "and the brokers too, bringing in their beach stuff on Fridays, parking the bags under their desks They were heading for the Hamptons or Fire Island. You and I were driving to Wrightsville." Her eyes meet mine for a moment, then glance away. "Those are good memories."

I should go. I desperately want to. My brain feels like it's releasing vapor. Can I say anything more? Any stunt to pull? Any emotion to appeal to?

Lesley has stepped another pace away, moving behind the chopping block against which the axe is resting.

"Is there anything I can get you?" Her hand elevates toward the porch. "Iced tea? I can put it in a jar for you..."

"I'm good, thanks."

"Take care of yourself," I hear myself say.

I'm backing down the slope.

"You too," says my wife.

We part with twenty feet of space between us.

It's November. Ten days after that morning with Lesley. A year to the day, almost, since Hugh Reaves first took a chance on me.

I owe him.

I owe Burton Lines.

I owe everybody there who has been my friend.

I try to hang in, but the heart for driving has gone out of me. Everything I have loved about trucking, every dream I've embraced of the future, is now turned on its head.

I take a load of paper from Charlotte to Spotswood and a second from Burlington to Ancram, New York. At Darlington I trade the box trailer for a flatbed and run three loads of fertilizer in a row, deadheading back each time, from Richmond to various farm supply stores in North and South Carolina.

"The road" has become torture for me. Miles on an odometer. What are the numbers ticking over except a false exercise in "getting somewhere"? Why am I doing this? Where do I imagine I'm going?

I'm not a driver. I'm an insult to the profession. Hugh Reaves was brave but foolish to stick his neck out for me. What is my problem? What brainless saga am I acting out inside my skull?

I repeat to myself for the thousandth time that I owe Hugh Reaves and I owe Burton Lines. I do. I owe Harold. I owe Sammy. I owe Byron and Ernie and Buddy. I owe Charley Stewart. I can't allow myself to cave like this. I can hang on. I have to hang on. I'm in a bad patch, that's all. I attached my hopes to some numb-nuts dream of winning back my wife. I'm an idiot.

Hang in.

Don't quit.

You can do it.

Just get through this rough place.

But four days later I walk into Hugh Reaves' office like a dog and tell him I'm quitting. Not in two weeks. Now. I'm too ashamed to stick around even to say thanks to Harold or Sammy when they get back in or to cross the yard for Buddy or Ernie or Charley Stewart. I stop only to see Bruce in Simpkinsville to thank him for being a friend and for taking me in to the fellowship, so he won't worry when he doesn't see me.

I don't say goodbye to 306-T.

I'm out of town and on the road, heading for Tinsley Oilfield Maintenance in Buras, Louisiana.

Book Two

JOHN FROM SEATTLE

Before I leave for Washington State, I sit down with Mo and explain my plan. I spread a Sunoco map on the carpet and trace the route I intend to take. My cat and I are camped in the guest house my friend Tony is renting on Jacks Peak in Monterey, California. Tony will be taking care of Mo while I'm gone.

I take Mo through my projected route... east and north out of Salinas to San Juan Bautista and Los Banos and then onto Interstate 5 heading straight north. I will pass San Francisco on the east side of the bay, continuing beyond Sacramento through the Alexander Valley, then Napa and Sonoma, through the Okanagan Valley in Oregon, then along 97 through Yakima, Washington trending east toward Spokane. I get out a calendar and explain to Mo, turning the pages, that I'll be gone six to eight weeks. That's how long the season lasts, or so I've been told by locals who've done it.

I'm going north to pick apples.

I can tell Mo isn't getting it. Or maybe he's getting it too well. He keeps turning away. His eyes refuse to meet mine.

It's four years since I bolted from Burton Lines. I've been back and forth across the country three times in that interval. The odometer on my van has just ticked past 273,000.

I'm writing. I've been working on a book full time for twenty months. I figure two more and it's done. But I'm running out of money. That's why I'm heading north for the apple season.

I explain to Mo that we need money. "I'll be back. I promise. You know I love you. Don't give Tony a hard time, okay?"

In fact, my savings have run out six months earlier. I've had to go back to work more than once in that interval.

Scouring the Help Wanted ads in the *Monterey Peninsula Herald* twenty weeks ago I find a trucking owner-operator—actually a couple, Mary and Mike Lukich of Seaside—who own three White Freightliners. They've got drivers for the first two but are looking for one for the third.

I interview in the living room of their house a few miles south of Fort Ord. Mary and Mike explain that they don't drive anymore themselves; they gave it up when they turned sixty. They contract their three Freightliners with a brokerage service. The service matches companies in need of transport with independent owners who have permits in all states and Canada. If Mary and Mike hire me as a driver, I will phone in to the brokerage after delivering each load. The dispatcher will tell me where to pick up the next one. It might be in the next county or it could be three states away. Pay is fifty-five cents a mile, loaded or dead-head. I'm thinking three or four months should give me enough cash to finish the book.

"If you'll take me, I'm in."

Mary and Mike pair me with another young trucker named Chris Harmon. We'll drive as a team. Chris is fresh out of Attica, the prison. Second-degree murder. Chris has a new wife and a baby. He's committed to going straight. That's good enough for Mary and Mike, and it's good enough for me. It's do or die for both of us.

We stay out nine weeks, Chris and I, with one turnaround.

At that point, Mike phones to tell us he has sold our truck.

The new owner will drive it himself, Mike says, so our employment is terminated.

Mike apologizes. It's business, he says. Chris and I are in Parma, Idaho, when the call comes in, having just picked up a load of potatoes in cardboard cartons bound for Adelphia, Wisconsin, where they will be processed into frozen crinkle-cuts. "Finish that delivery," says Mike. He instructs us to deadhead from Wisconsin to Lorain, Ohio, and there hand over the Freightliner to its new owner. Mike promises to wire Chris and me bus fare home.

Chris takes the termination hard. For two days he talks about nothing but killing Mike. He's serious. He acknowledges that he'll have to kill me too since I'm a witness to his intentions. He tells me how he would track me down. "Someone like you," he says. "I know where you'd be. Around some college town or some hippie place like San Francisco."

He'd stake out likely venues, Chris declares, until he found me, then he'd beat me to death with a baseball bat.

Why a baseball bat, I ask.

"Because you can burn it and leave no weapon for the law to trace."

I reason with Chris over truck-stop helpings of apple pie and ice cream, trying to get him to rethink this whole project. I don't really believe he'll come after me, but I'm seriously concerned for Mike. I appeal to Chris on behalf of his new wife and child. No dent. What finally gets through is his fish. Chris has just spent three hundred dollars on an aquarium for tropical fish. He loves them. "What's gonna happen to your fish, Chris, if you have to go back to prison or even just stand trial?"

Chris takes his bus ticket and heads home. I drive on to Lorain, drop off the truck, then hitchhike back to California. The twenty-seven bucks that would've gone to Greyhound goes into my pocket.

That's when the idea of picking apples comes up. I could go back to New York and find work in advertising. That's how I had saved the twenty-seven hundred dollars that I've been living on for twenty-two months. But I'm afraid if I do that, I'll get sucked into the real world and crap out on finishing this book.

That is an outcome too hideous to contemplate.

34. MIGRANT LABOR

The first day at the orchard we come upon a dead body. I've been in Washington State four days now, first in Trinidad, then Wenatchee, now in Chelan. I've scouted three other orchards in the valley before a girl at County Employment sends me to a place called Beebe's. The pickers at the first three orchards, and the others before that, were either from local jails or guys with milky eyes and no teeth who manage somehow to pass out drunk by two in the afternoon.

I meet a man named John, from Seattle, outside the County office. He confirms the employment lady's recommendation. "I've worked every orchard in the state. Trust me, for living conditions and length of season, Beebe's is as good as you'll find."

John is about twenty years older than me with a salt-and-pepper crew cut and a face burnt brown as saddle leather. The tattoo on his right forearm says

USMC

beneath a drawing of a bulldog wearing a World War I-type helmet.

John explains that not every orchard offers work that runs the full eight-week season. Beebe's does. "You don't want to sign on to an orchard that cuts out halfway through. Then you're back on the tramp when every season-long place is full up with pickers."

Something about John reminds me of Hugh Reaves. I invite him to toss his pack into the back of my van.

Whichever orchard he decides on, I'm sticking with him.

We head for Beebe's. The dead body is laid out on a canvas sheet on the grass outside a line of six paint-peeling bunkhouses. The fellow was a migrant fruit picker, unidentified so far. Cops from Wenatchee have come out, in two cruisers, along with a paramedic van from the Chelan Fire Department.

"What killed him?" John asks. The dead man looks to be about sixty. There's no blood and no apparent trauma.

The medic shrugs. "People die."

An orchard foreman asks me and John to help him get rid of the mattress the man was sleeping on when he died. John's glance to me says, *Say yes.* He and I drag the thing out back into a weedy field to a pile of half a dozen other pallets, several semi-charred for some reason, three with visible blood stains.

I ask the foreman if people die a lot out here. "First one this season," he says. His name is Boros, though he doesn't tell us that then. He thanks John and tells us to find a bunkhouse we like—nine of them sit all in a row—and make ourselves at home. "Wait up!" And he hands us each a chit for an extra dessert at the mess hall.

We've missed the first week of the season. John confirms this when I drive him into town that night to get some batteries for his transistor radio. "The Romes are over. Red Deliciouses start tomorrow."

John can see from my face I'm a little uneasy with dead guys popping up and the general down-and-out aspect of the situation. "Stick around," he says. "It's not as creepy as it seems... or it won't be once the work starts. The crazy ones pull the pin early. Who's left are good people.

"It's pretty much fruit tramps doing this work," John tells me as we drive back to the orchard. "Lot of 'em riding the rails like the old days." He himself comes out every year from Seattle, where he lives in a single-room-occupancy hotel. He can make enough in a season here, he says, to last the rest of the year, counting his pension and disability. John is missing teeth too, but they're in the back of his mouth. "You know the definition of a tramp?" he asks me.

A tramp is an itinerant worker.

A hobo is an itinerant nonworker.

A bum is a nonitinerant nonworker.

John picks the third bunkhouse south of the chow hall. It seems in the best repair. I take the bunk next to the one he chooses. They're all single racks, no double-deckers. "Guys roll out of the upper story drunk and break their necks," John says.

By the end of the first week of Red Deliciouses, the bunkhouses have all filled. No black guys. Not a one. No Hispanics. It's all whites and American Indians and, as John said, all tramps.

I'm the only person with a vehicle. Each evening I haul a load of guys into Chelan, to the Safeway, the laundromat, or just to get a bottle and a pack of smokes. John never goes. He stays by himself on the orchard. He doesn't drink, though I have overheard him talking to Marvin, a Kootenai Indian from Flathead Lake, Montana, to the effect that year-round except during the season, he kills enough wine each night to pass out.

John is also the fastest and most accomplished picker.

A season in apples, I'm learning, starts with the Romes. These are cooking apples, red and round. Different types of apples come into season in different weeks. The tramps and trucks move from one section of the orchard to another, picking the rows clean as they go.

The way you pick apples is with a canvas sack that you wear across your chest like a vest. Straps go around your shoulders. The top of the sack is held open by a heavy wire rim. That's where you put the apples. The bottom is open. A heavy cord hangs from each corner. The cord has knots at three places—top, middle, and bottom. Hooks on the sack catch the knots.

You tuck the open bottom under when you're ready to start picking. Now your sack has a sealed floor. As you fill the pack with apples, you re-hook the knotted line farther down. By the time you're full, the bag hangs to your knees. Climb down your ladder—with the sack outboard so you don't fall—and cross to your bin. Bend over the rail with your chest-pack in front of you. Lay its canvas bottom on the floor of the bin or atop the pile of apples you've picked so far and unhook the knotted lines. The belly of the sack opens. Out tumble the apples. Be gentle! If the foreman sees you bruise the fruit, he'll throw them out and throw you out too if you do it a second time.

You pick apples from a tall aluminum ladder whose rails taper inward from bottom to top. It's a strong, industrial-grade instrument. You lean it in, hard, up to the crown of the tree. You collect your apples in stout wooden bins. The bins are four feet by four, three feet deep. The orchard sets them out on pallets in the lanes between the trees. Gas-powered forklifts pick them up when they're full. Each picker gets a round of bins. Numbers are stenciled on the side. At the end of the day, you get credited for the number of bins you've picked.

The work is hard. Pickers drop out every day. The orchard has an incentive system to keep you from bolting. For each bin you pick, the office records one bonus dollar in your account, above and beyond the four bucks you've officially earned for that bin. If you stay through the end of the season, you get those accumulated dollars in one final bonus.

There are fast pickers and slow pickers. John is the fastest. He has been doing this, "coming out for the apples," for twenty-five years. I fall in beside him in the chow line at the end of the first day. We're sidestepping down a steam table manned by women and girls from the owner's family and the orchard's year-round employees. "Like Parris Island, ain't it?" says John. I ask him how many bins he got today.

"Ten."

Wow.

He asks how I made out.

"Three. Barely."

I ask him what's his record.

"Twelve."

At the table John hands me a five and asks me to pick him up a carton of Camels when I go into town.

"Come in with me," I say. "We'll stop at the Dairy Queen and get a shake."

"I stay here."

"Why?"

"It's better."

One of the other super-fast pickers is a guy named Clayton from Oklahoma. He looks exactly like Steve McQueen except he has no teeth past the upper bicuspid on his left side. He knows John from years back. "The cherries. Peaches. We been everywhere."

He tells me John is the only guy he's ever known who can turn himself off alcohol "like flipping a switch."

"That's why he won't go into town?"

"John was married to this gal," Clayton says, and he names an actress I've seen in half a dozen movies.

"Don't shit me."

"That's what I thought too. Then one day in Seattle he shows up with her. I about crapped my pants."

"Is he still married to her?"

Clayton gives me a look. "Living in an SRO hotel on Skid Row?"

35. ALL I KNOW HOW TO DO IS WORK

On the orchard nobody asks about your business. It's a matter of respect. That you're here in these bunkhouses says all anyone needs to know.

For my part I don't want to talk.

I'm here for money. I'm here to bust my ass for as long as it takes and head back south with enough of a stash to finish my book or get as close as I can.

The book is about Burton Lines. I started it in New York when I was working at an ad agency. The book is about Hugh Reaves and Harold and Byron... and Lesley.

Do I have any idea what a novel is? Fuck no. I have no concept of theme or narrative device or crisis/climax/resolution. I don't know what a character is. I have never heard of three-act structure, Inciting Incident, or All is Lost moment.

All I know how to do is work. I drove out to California from New York twenty-two months ago and found a little house behind a bigger house in Carmel Valley for one hundred bucks a month. I opened an account at the Bank of America and put in my savings—twenty-seven hundred dollars. Each Monday I walk into the bank and cash a check for twenty-five dollars. That lasts me all week.

I get up at five and make myself a gigantic breakfast to power myself through the day. I'm alone. I have no friends. I have no girlfriend. For breakfast I don't have sausage or bacon. I have liver. I want the power. I'm not here to fuck around. I will finish this book or kill myself trying.

I write on my Smith-Corona typewriter. I have dragged this ancient monster out from its nest beneath three feet of junk in the back of my van and set it up on the kitchen table in the back room of my little house. The typewriter is a manual. This is good. For a beginner like me, it's indispensable training. I revise paragraphs ten times, twenty times. I have to just because it takes me that long to type them without mistakes.

I worked to save money, as I said, for an ad agency in Manhattan, my second time around. My job title there was copywriter. I wrote ads and TV commercials. I wasn't particularly good at it. I try as hard as I can, but my stuff is nowhere near as quirky or inventive as writers who are seriously talented.

All I know how to do is work.

Before I got the ad job, I drove a cab. I still had my typewriter but, just like at Burton Lines, I never took it out. I wasn't even sure where I had stashed it. Then one night something happened.

Here's the passage from *The War of Art* (2002).

> I washed up in New York a couple of decades ago, making twenty bucks a night driving a cab and running away full-time from doing my work. One night, alone in my $110-a-month sublet, I hit bottom in terms of having diverted myself into so many phony channels so many times that I couldn't rationalize it for one more evening. I dragged out my ancient Smith-Corona, dreading the experience as pointless, fruitless, meaningless, not to say the most painful exercise I could think of. For two hours I made myself sit there, torturing out some trash that I chucked immediately into the shitcan. That was enough. I put the machine away. I went back to the kitchen. In the sink sat ten days of dishes. For some reason I had enough excess energy that I decided to wash them. The warm

water felt pretty good. The soap and sponge were doing their thing. A pile of clean plates began rising in the drying rack. To my amazement I realized I was whistling.

It hit me that I had turned a corner.

I was okay.

I would be okay from here on.

It wasn't like I could suddenly write. I couldn't. It would be years, even decades, I could tell, before I might produce anything good, if that day ever came at all.

But finally, after years of running from it, I had at last sat down and done my work.

I began writing in earnest. Not a book, not a story. Just pages. Keystrokes on paper. To this day, I have no idea what I wrote then. All I know is it worked to quell my mania. I sat down crazy and I got up sane.

It's winter in Manhattan. I can't remember the year. Five in the evening, dark. I'm heading out to the subway to ride up to the Bronx for my taxi job. It's snowing, which is great for driving a hack. People are desperate for a ride. Big tips.

I come down my steps. A young mom with two small kids is wrangling suitcases and blankets on a stoop across the street. I go over. She's being evicted.

Short version: I give her my keys.

"Take my bedroom. I'll sleep in the other room. There's food in the fridge. I'll see you when I get off work."

The girl's name is Penny. She's from Canada. Her life is even more screwed up than mine. Her husband took off and left her with thousands of dollars of debt. She works as a medical secretary at St. Vincent's in the West Village. Her wages are being garnished. She brings home next to nothing, and the situation is not going to change for years.

So now I'm supporting a divorcee and two sprouts.

The relationship is chaste. I'm way too guilty to take advantage of a woman in desperate straits. Plus I'm still excruciatingly in love with Lesley.

After school I read to the kids. They have no idea they're broke or that their mom is half a step from the poorhouse. The one book I have with illustrations is *Moby Dick*. Marina, who's three, takes a shine to "Captain Hathead." I must say the woodcut illustrations are terrific. Who knew Herman Melville had an appeal to three-year-olds?

Here's my day. Home at three in the morning after my six-to-two shift. Up at six for breakfast with Penny and the kids. She takes Alec to school and Marina to day care. I sleep till noon, then get up and sit down at the typewriter.

My writing has acquired an intention. I'm working on a novel about Burton Lines. I pick up Marina at three-thirty. Alec finds his own way home. Penny's back by five. We pass in the hall as I head out to the cab company.

Six months in with Penny, I find work at the ad agency. By now the kids are so attached to me, and me to them, that the idea of being separated is inconceivable. Then one spring morning the bell rings. It's Penny's husband. From her stories I had expected Crazy Joe Gallo. But he turns out to be a nice guy, from Alberta like Penny. He's tall and handsome. Clearly Penny is still in love with him.

He moves in too.

Penny won't let her husband into her bed, so I give him a third room, a storage cubby for the real tenant's painting canvases. The husband's name is Jean-Luc. He goes by Luke. He's got a degree in drama from McGill in Montreal, but he makes a living as an airplane mechanic for

Eastern, maintaining Lockheed Super-Constellations on the eight-to-four shift at LaGuardia.

Luke is an actor. Days, he goes on auditions. One night on his way out he asks what I'm writing. I give him a few pages. He takes them with him to work. When he comes home, he's ecstatic. "This shit is great! What are you doing with it? Can I show it to the director I'm working with?"

Three months later I'm sitting in the audience with Penny and Alec and Marina as Luke knocks 'em dead in a church-basement Off-Off Broadway production of a one-act play written by the director based on the few pages I passed to Luke on his way to work.

Two months after that Luke gets a part on a soap and the family, reunited, moves into a duplex in Astoria.

I'm shattered. Losing the kids. What the fuck?

The solitary plus of this fiasco is I acquire an agent. Her name is Radmila. She's Luke's agent. She's sixty-three and from Yugoslavia. She's also a psychic. She has a call-in show from eleven to midnight three nights a week on WBAM from the Brooklyn Academy of Music. Over cheeseburgers at the Empire Diner, Radmila asks me how soon I can finish "this truck-driving book." I tell her I've got almost three grand saved from my ad job. I can live for a year on that. I'm about to quit and move someplace cheap where I can concentrate on nothing but the book.

Radmila gives me the long once-over. "Luke tells me you've never finished anything. Can I count on you?"

"You're the psychic. You tell me."

Radmila apologizes. She picks up the tab. Outside she informs me as gently as she can that she has to let me go as a client. "It's business. You understand."

Radmila sets a hand on my arm. "You will make it as a writer," she declares, "but only after lengthy trials and abundant heartbreak."

36. A BIN AND A HUMP

The next day I get four bins with a quarter hump. A hump is a partial bin that the forklifts set aside under the trees and you top off the next day. John gets ten bins that day. The day after, with my quarter-bin head start, I still only finish with four. John gets eleven.

"How many apples are you picking with each hand?" He means each time I reach up. I tell the truth. "One."

"Come on," John says. His look of disappointment stings. We're sitting, after evening chow, on the weathered pine stoop of the bunkhouse with Marvin from Flathead Lake and Clayton from Oklahoma. I know from watching John work that he gets three apples in each hand and sometimes four.

"Try for two tomorrow," he says. "Put your mind to it."

John demonstrates with his right hand and left extended. "Get the first apple with your thumb, forefinger, and middle finger. Use your index finger and thumb to hold this first one in place. Then get the second with your middle finger and your fourth and fifth. Focus on your right hand first. You can do it. Once you get the hang, try it with your left. It'll be hard, but what's the point of doing anything if you're not trying to get better? Now each time you reach up to a limb you're bringing in four apples instead of two. That's how you fill a bin, brother. That's how you make money."

The next day I take a break, twice, just to watch John work. Somebody should film him, that's how beautiful he is. No rush. No hurry. He's fifteen feet up on his ladder, deep into the crown of the tree. His right hand extends into the thicket of green. One apple, two, three; meanwhile his left is doing the same. It's a rhythm. His hands drop to the sack across his chest, gently depositing the fruit so it doesn't bruise, then back up into the tree again for another three in each hand. In ninety seconds, he's filled his bag. Down to the bin, roll them out, back up to the branches and do it again, six hours, eight hours, ten.

37. A KNIGHT

Mornings on the orchard start an hour before dawn. Breakfast is at five-thirty, with steel trays and chipped beef on toast. A sign says:

TAKE ALL YOU WANT BUT EAT ALL YOU TAKE

You're on your ladder while it's still dark. You want to be. The longer the day, the more bins you can pick.

Each morning more guys go missing. They've taken off during the night.

Who are these tramps? Most of the white guys come out from Seattle. The Indians are more local. They come to Beebe's orchard every year. Most go south from here for the cherries and then on to Arizona for whatever they pick down there. They keep in touch over the year, not just with each other, but with the orchards and ranches. They come from SRO hotels on or around Skid Row. Seattle, John tells me, is where the name Skid Row comes from. "The street originally was called Skid Road, from the skids that timber would be dragged on to the lumber mills."

John, as I said, has stopped drinking for the work season. "How do you do that?" Marvin asks.

John taps his temple.

Lunch in the orchards is a paper sack from the chow hall with two bologna and cheese sandwiches on white bread with a bag of chips and a hard-boiled egg. You wolf it under the trees, adding an apple or two from our own bag, so you can get back on your ladder and keep picking.

One lunch, two weeks in, John alludes to something about his service in Korea in 1950. I ask him, just talking, if he was at the Chosin Reservoir.

He nods.

A regiment of Marines—about three thousand men—held off ninety thousand soldiers of the Chinese Ninth Army for two weeks in temperatures that dropped to forty below zero. Loading the bodies of their fellow Marines onto trucks, men had to literally snap the frozen limbs off some, to make room to carry them all.

"You were there?"

John's eyes answer.

My friend has just vaulted into the pantheon. He is a Spartan from Thermopylae, an Englishman of Agincourt. "What was it like?" I ask dumbly.

"Cold."

If he had spoken a single word more, I would not have believed him.

All John has to say is one word, "Chosin," and he is a Jedi knight to me.

38. FRUIT TRAMPS

Our bunkhouse started with fourteen guys. By mid-October we're down to six—John and me, Marvin from Flathead Lake, Clayton from Oklahoma, and two brothers, Leon and Cleon, from Visalia, California, who stow their gear in the bunkhouse but have not slept in their racks a single night or showed up once for breakfast. They appear on their ladders every morning as the sun's first rays peek through.

Marvin is a tribal Kootenai. Of course, the tramps call him "Chief."

"What kind of Indian are you, Chief?" one toothless migrant asks Marvin outside the chow hall.

"My mother was a Washington Redskin, and my father was a Cleveland Indian."

Marvin doesn't like being asked that question. It pisses the hell out of him being called Chief.

Each morning Marvin's pillow is splotched with blood that he hacks up during the night. I take him into town to the laundromat to wash the pillowcases, but the stain is deep into the filling of the pillow itself, and it gets bigger every morning.

How would I characterize these gentlemen of the highway? To a man they are wonderful guys. They're funny. They're kind. They'll share their last cigarette or lend you their final dollar. They are not lazy. Without exception they're hard workers. They can go all day in cold, heat, rain, and never complain. Yet it's clear no few live right on the edge. They remind me a little of Chris from Attica. They're good until they're not. You don't want to be around when they go off.

I ask John one evening if he has ever thought about putting something on paper about Chosin. He laughs. "Visit me in Seattle sometime. I got a trunk full to the top."

"John! You gotta do something with it!"

"I'll leave that to you, little brother."

John is the only one who knows what I'm doing down in California.

"I'm serious, John. I'll bet there's some great shit in that trunk."

"Maybe."

"Well?"

He laughs again. "I'll leave that to you."

John continues to tutor me on picking technique. Each apple must be twisted off its spur on the tree, leaving the stem in the apple. You can't just jerk. A stemless apple will go mealy in storage. If Boros or any of the other foremen catch you binning fruit without stems, they'll can you and you'll lose your bonus. "Are you getting two with each hand now?" John asks me. When I answer, "Sometimes," he gives me a dark look.

"Come on," he says. "That's unacceptable."

John says he saw me yesterday having a smoke as the sun was setting.

"What?" I say. "Don't you get tired?"

"Of course," he says. And he gives me that look.

Once a week John comes into town with me to the laundromat. We get a couple of shakes from the DQ and sit on benches out back looking over the parking lot.

"What are you gonna do with this book once you finish," he asks.

"Try to sell it."

"And if you can't?"

"Save money again and write another."

"Why?"

I hesitate.

"You're not trying to prove something to somebody?"

I look away.

"Fool's errand," says John.

I don't quite hear him.

"Fool's errand," he repeats.

John reaches across. With one forefinger he taps my forehead.

"Here," he says.

"What?"

"You heard me."

I stop at a pay phone to call my landlady in California. I'm working, I assure her. I'm saving money. "See you in three weeks. Don't rent the place to anyone else."

John and I eat together each night, with Clayton and Marvin, at the same table in the chow hall. I ask John what he thinks about his fellow tramps. Why do they come out on the road every year, beyond trying to put away a few bucks? Why does *he* come out?

"Migration," John answers without hesitation. "It's in the blood. Birds migrate. Fish. Buffalo. In Africa, the great herds follow the same trails every year."

Marvin nods in agreement. "The tribes lived on this land for ten thousand years. They followed the game and the grass."

"What about you?" Clayton addresses me directly. "Tell the truth. You love this shit. You ain't here by accident." Everyone laughs. "This is the secret nobody says out loud. The modern world sucks. A job? A wife? What's so fucking great about that? Kids? Come on. If I was back in medieval times, I'd be on the tramp just like now. Hey, farmer, got work for us? Fight a war. Harvest a field. It's in the DNA. I know this road life's hard. I seen all of it. But I pass along a street of houses in a town and all I can do is feel sorry for those motherfuckers."

Clayton, as I said, is the second-fastest picker behind John. He looks like a compact version of Steve McQueen and has no small share of the same charisma. "I'm a mechanic by trade," he says. "Been working on cars and trucks my whole life. My family back in Enid's been begging me for years to come in off the road. Last Thanksgiving I did. My uncle gave me a job in his shop. Skilled work, good money. I found me a house, even had a pretty little girlfriend."

"What happened?" Marvin asks.

Clayton pauses, dragging on a Lucky Strike.

"Three months. Couldn't take it no more. Pulled the pin."

Book Three

PAUL RINK

Quitting the season early is called "pulling the pin." The phrase, as John explains, comes from riding the rails. To uncouple one freight car from another, the trainman pulls out a heavy steel pin.

In the bunkhouse you wake up and one of the racks is unslept in.

"What happened to Harry?"

"He pulled the pin."

I understand pulling the pin. I pulled the pin on my first book. I pulled the pin on my marriage. I pulled the pin on Hugh Reaves and Burton Lines. I have never undertaken anything in my life that didn't end with me pulling the pin.

I am determined, now, *not* to pull the pin.

When I came out to California from New York twenty-two months ago, I had twenty-seven hundred dollars in savings from my advertising job. That money is to finish my trucking book.

I will finish that sonofabitch or kill myself trying.

My body is here on the orchard but every other part of me is back in Carmel Valley in my little rented house behind the bigger house.

In my little house I have my worktable, I have my Smith-Corona, my mattress, my box springs, my bed frame. I have a couch I found on the street in Pacific Grove. I have kitchen utensils—a pot, a teakettle, a frying pan. I have one spoon and one fork. I have a knife.

I have no TV, no radio, no stereo. This is before computers, so no email, no Instagram, no social media.

I have no correspondents. I write to nobody—not friends, not family. Nobody. And nobody writes to me.

My day goes like this. I wake before dawn, eat a breakfast for a lumberjack. Four eggs, raw milk, potatoes, tomatoes. Bacon or sausage are too weak for me. Liver. A big slab for power. I walk for an hour. The sun is coming up now.

I have a friend and mentor, a writer named Paul Rink, who lives down River Road in his camper/pickup that he calls "Moby Dick." Actually Paul has a house—the camper is parked in the street out front—but he prefers the camper. He only goes into the house to pee.

Every morning I visit with Paul. Paul makes ranch coffee, meaning he dumps raw grounds into a saucepan that has been used for this purpose and no other for so long its bowl is half an inch thick with calcified coffee sludge. The only way the human palate can endure this level of acidity is to lace the brew with sugar in great whacking wads.

Paul talks to me about writers. He has known Steinbeck from Salinas. He lived two doors down from Henry Miller on Partington Ridge in Big Sur. Paul turns me on to authors I have never heard of. Or, if I've heard of them, I've never had the guts to actually read them. The Greeks: Homer, Herodotus, Thucydides, Xenophon, Plato, Aeschylus, Sophocles, Euripides, Aristophanes. The Romans: Caesar, Livy, Cicero, Seneca, Epictetus, Marcus Aurelius.

Paul makes me read Flaubert and Victor Hugo, Montaigne and La Rochefoucauld. He insists I read Sartre and Simone de Beauvoir, Knut Hamsun, Andre Malraux, Giuseppe Lampedusa, Jean Rhys, Italo Calvino, Laurens van der Post. I must imbibe the full modern canon—Tolstoy, Dostoevsky, Chekhov, Turgenev, Stendhal, Victor Hugo, Hawthorne, Melville, Hemingway, Fitzgerald, Japanese writers, Chinese writers.

Paul lectures me on self-discipline. Nothing else counts but getting your pages every day. Be ruthless with yourself. This is life or death. Don't kid yourself that it's anything else.

Paul doesn't admire writers personally. "The ones I've known are mostly self-involved pricks and egomaniacs. I don't condemn them. It's the agony of the process. I wouldn't want a son or daughter of mine to write. I would try to talk you out of it too, Steve, but I can see there's no chance of that."

In New Orleans, I lived in a neighborhood where the streets were named after the Muses. Thalia Street, Calliope, Erato, Clio, Euterpe, Melpomene, Urania, Polyhymnia, Terpsichore. It was a maritime neighborhood, with boarding houses for merchant seamen and other transient laborers of the port. I tramped up and down those lanes every day, but I never thought about the reality of the goddesses' existence, and it had certainly never occurred to me to revere them or to attempt to invoke their favor.

Paul changes this. He teaches me the prayer that he himself recites every morning before he sits down to work.

"It's the Invocation of the Muse, from Homer's Odyssey, the T.E. Lawrence translation." T.E. Lawrence meaning Lawrence of Arabia, among whose many Oxford-spawned passions was a deep love for the classics.

"This is how the Odyssey starts. The first eleven lines. It's Homer offering his prayer to the goddess before he begins to sing. Remember," Paul says, "the Odyssey was originally sung, not written."

O divine Poesy, Goddess, Daughter of Zeus,
Sustain for me this song of the various-minded man,
who, after he had plundered the innermost citadel of
hallowed Troy, was made to stray grievously about the
coasts of men, the sport of their customs, good and bad,
while his heart, through all the seafaring, ached with
an agony to redeem himself and bring his company
safe home. Vain hope! For them! To destroy for meat
the oxen of the most exalted sun, wherefore the
Sun God blotted out the day of their return.

Make this tale live for us in all its many
bearings, O Muse!

"The Odyssey begins with a crime," Paul observes. "'... after he had plundered the innermost citadel of hallowed Troy.'

"Note the word 'hallowed.' In the flush of victory, Odysseus breaks into the sacred precinct of the goddess and pillages it. An outrage against heaven. That's you and me, Steve. That's everybody. We have committed a crime against ourselves or against the primal order of the universe, and for this heaven has cast us out and set us in exile upon our journey."

Paul has a theory that all stories are about exile. "Exile," he says, "is the essence of the human condition. Animals are not in exile. Only us. Every hero or heroine you write must be in exile—from God and from themselves."

Paul is a great reader of Carl Jung. He assigns me *Man and his Symbols* and *The Archetypes and the Collective Unconscious*. He gives me his own copy of *Memories, Dreams, Reflections*.

"I don't know what you're writing, Steve. I don't want to know. I'll never read it. I'll never judge it. All I ask of it, and of you, is that it come from that sacred space inside you and that it stay true, as you write it, to the ideals of that hallowed precinct."

On his manual Remington, Paul types out Homer's Invocation of the Muse and gifts it to me. I still have it. Long ago the page disintegrated into four quadrants. The type is so faded now I can't tell which part of the prayer is which, or which verses reside beneath my various coffee spills and ink splotches and oily fingerprints.

In my little house behind the big house, I have two rooms. The front holds the kitchen and bedroom, all in one space. The back is where I work. The floor is painted concrete. The rear wall butts up to a hillside. It's cold. In the winter, *really* cold. I have a gas heater in the front room, a square metal box the size of a refrigerator. I work in the back room until my hands are so stiff I can't feel my fingers on the typewriter keys. Then I go out front, turn on the heater and stand over it till sensation returns. I turn off the flame to save money and go back to work.

My cat Mo lives with me in the little house behind the big house. His perch is on my worktable. He sprawls on his side with his back resting against the left wall of the typewriter. The carriage passes over his head, back and forth as I type. Mo doesn't seem to mind.

I write all day. I have no idea what I'm doing. I have never heard of narrative structure or theme or concept or act 1, act 2, act 3. I work entirely on instinct. I'm writing, as I said, about Burton Lines, about the trucking company. I'm writing about myself.

A typewriter is not a digital instrument. When you make a mistake, you can't correct it. You can't move blocks of text around. You can't check spelling or grammar. You can't save what you write. If you want to make a copy, you stick a sheet of carbon paper between your top page and the page that will become your copy. To edit, you get out the scissors and Scotch tape and patch together a paragraph from Section X with another from Section Y. The exercise is preposterously inefficient. But there's one great thing about working on a typewriter.

At the end of the day, you have pages. Actual physical pages that you have created.

I work for twenty-two months without a break. My routine never varies. The only entertainment in my schedule is a movie once a week. Two former actors, lovers for fifty years, have created a charming local theater under California live oaks. It's called the Tantamount. It's only open Saturdays. "How I envy you," the white-haired actor/host declaims to us in the audience as he introduces tonight's showing of *Ninotchka*. "Seeing Garbo for the first time! Feel free, please, to fall in love!"

And I read. I write all day and read all night. The village has a tiny satellite library stocked with a couple of hundred books, mostly children's stories and cookbooks. But you can put in an order to the county system with branches in Monterey and Salinas. The books show up three or four days later. It's a great system.

I read *War and Peace*, I read *Madame Bovary*, I read *Fathers and Sons*, *The Red and the Black*, *Crime and Punishment*, *The Brothers Karamazov*. I read *Hunger*, *Anna Karenina*, *Don Quixote*. I read *Tropic of Cancer* and *Tropic of Capricorn*, *Sexus*, *Nexus*, *Plexus*, *Quiet Days in Clichy*. I read *Big Sur and the Oranges of Hieronymus Bosch*. My friend Paul is a character in this one.

I read everything you're supposed to read in high school and college but never do, or if you do, you're so psyched to read to the test that you don't learn a damn thing. Am I learning anything now? Fuck no. The books pass through my consciousness like sunlight through glass. I don't care. They're in my cells now. I love them. Their impress has etched itself in some occult recess of my heart.

I wish every aspiring writer or artist could have a year or two years like this—a season when you have no responsibilities except to your own Muse and your own daimon, a run of months when you're invisible to everybody but yourself, when you don't give a shit about anything except the challenge before you, when you could drop dead on the street and no one would stop except to step over your cold corpse, and you don't care.

Shame drove me through those twenty-two months, as I said, but the inner journey and internal transformation ran far deeper, even though I didn't know it then and couldn't have articulated it if my life had depended upon it. There are gods who watch over lost souls, particularly those who dream, and when these divinities' unknowable purposes align with the enterprise of these exiled souls, a force begins to flow that is as unquenchable as it is pure, and as knowing as it is indefatigable.

When you're alone with your solitary obsession, each day builds upon the one before. Energy concentrates. Your passion and intensity create a planet all your own, like the one the Little Prince lived on in Saint-Exupery's book. This planet possesses its own gravitational field, and that field draws unto itself like-minded particles from space, from the aether, from the Big Bang. I mean ideas. Ideas for scenes, for dialogue, for characters, for conflicts. This field draws phrases you have never spoken. It attracts words you never knew you knew.

On my little planet I don't read the news or listen to the radio. A bomb could go off down the street and I wouldn't hear it. My life is the world inside my head. Yeah, every now and then the odd female spends the night. But I eject her—nicely—in the morning. The only physical entity permitted on this planet is my cat.

My cat understands. One of the books I'm reading is Joshua Slocum's *Sailing Alone Around the World*. I'm sailing too. My cat is sailing with me. We are circumnavigating a globe that only he and I know, and the stakes are life and death. Sometimes I don't feed Mo for a week. He doesn't miss it. He hunts. He makes kills. He brings in birds and mice and stands over them with his paw on their necks. I praise him and make a fuss.

I'm hunting too. I'm making kills. I never show my pages to anyone. I never tell anyone except Paul what I'm doing on my little planet. Paul becomes superstitious in such moments. He doesn't want to jinx anything.

Paul introduces me to his New York literary agent, a Dutch gentleman of seventy years named Barthold Fles. Bart takes me on. Thirty-five years later, in *The Knowledge*, I fictionalize him as "Martin Fabrikant."

> Marty is a death camp survivor. He's got the tattoo.
> He never speaks about the experience directly (I only
> know him through my friend Pablo, who originally

introduced me to Marty) but he'll make remarks from time to time whose gist is, "Appreciate life. Never complain. Work hard and do your best."

Marty has one other mantra: "Talent is bullshit."

"I've seen a million writers with talent. It means nothing. You need guts, you need stick-to-it-iveness. It's work, you gotta work. That's why you're gonna make it, son. You work. No one can take that away from you.

"And I'll tell you something else," Marty says. "Appreciate these days. These days when you're broke and struggling, they're the best days of your life. You're gonna break through, my boy. And when you do, you'll look back on this time and think this is when I was really an artist, when everything was pure and I had nothing but the dream and the work. Enjoy it now. Pay attention. These are the good days. Be grateful for them."

I do my reading in bed at night in my little house with a single lamp and my head propped on a doubled-over pillow. Mo parks himself just above and behind me, on the windowsill. He likes watching the pages flip. No few times I have found myself turning back toward him, wondering if he is reading along.

As I write this now, almost two generations have passed. Yet the weeks and months of that time remain vivid to me. Nothing in my life before or since has penetrated me like those two years. In our society we erect altars to love. Songs, movies, even TV commercials tell us love is the answer.

I don't believe it.

I believe in a different kind of love. I can't define it except to say that it has nothing to do with the flesh, nor is it particularly personal. The goddess is real. Her stream flows inside you and me like an underground river.

That river is our life, our real life.

During those two years I lived beside that river. Nothing came between me and it. Each morning I entered the river, and I didn't come out until I was so exhausted I could no longer swim or stand.

No one had told me about this river. No teacher had instructed me on it. No mentor had pointed me in its direction. I had tried before to enter this river, but I could never find the opening. Not like this time. Not like now. Was I producing anything of value? Not yet. That would come, if it ever did, years and decades in the future. But I was in the river and the river was in me.

The price of entrance to the river is work. Work is the toll of admission. The river can't turn you away as long as you're willing to pay. Paul would tell me that, and Bart too, and what they said was true. If you're willing to pay the freight, the river has to let you in. That's the law.

40. WHIPPOORWILL

When I was a kid, I worked as a caddie at a place called the Whippoorwill Club in Armonk, New York. Sounds dumb, I know, but this course was and is one of the primo designs in a three-cornered area—Westchester, Long Island, Connecticut—that has more golf courses per capita, and more quality challenges—Winged Foot (East and West), Shinnecock Hills, Bethpage Black, the National Golf Links, Maidstone, Westchester C.C., Inwood, Apawamis, Quaker Ridge, Piping Rock, Stanwich, Yale, Tamarack—than any comparable region in the country.

I started when I was eleven. We made four bucks a bag with a dollar tip to make five. Two bags equaled ten dollars. Two loops made twenty.

Why do kids caddie? For some it was money. Others were poor kids who wanted to go to college. Like in the movie *Caddyshack*, they'd suck up to certain club members—judges, lawyers, community leaders—angling for a letter or phone call that would one day open a door. Not me. For me, it was all about the game. About learning to play.

When I was twelve, I handed Frank the caddiemaster a list of my approved players. The list was hand-written, in pencil, on the back of a scorecard. Nobody does something like that. To my amazement, Frank accepted this. The list was the only golfers I wanted to caddie for. They were the best players at the club but, more importantly for me, they were the players with the most technically perfect swings.

I wanted to study them. I promised Frank I would give them my all. I idolized them. I revered them. Even when I was so undersized my nickname in the yard was "Shorty" (later "Peanuts"), Frank would send me out overloaded with the monster bags of Jack Hesler—former Kentucky State amateur champ and Junior Davis Cup tennis player—and

Brant Overstander—New York State high hurdles champion and plus-three handicapper, not to mention Hugh Skelly, Stu Benedict, and Sandy Piper.

If you were a golf-mad kid and your family belonged to a country club, you got to grow up taking lessons from the pro. For us caddies, the learning track was old school—find somebody great and study the hell out of them. On a typical round caddying for Hesler or Overstander, I would deliberately station myself behind, in front of, or to their right or left, so I could watch and imbibe specific aspects of their technique—footwork, turn, action through the ball. I studied their grips. I inhaled their attitudes. I missed nothing. How they handled adversity, how they seized opportunities, what phrases they muttered to themselves when they thought no one was listening.

The bond was by no means one-way. These athletes—and that's what they were—reckoned the look in my eyes and the eyes of my brother young caddies. They would turn to us in moments of competition when the idea of seeking counsel from a thirteen-year-old was patently ridiculous, and they'd pay us the compliment of taking us seriously. We would have thrown ourselves into fire for them. When the big tri-state tournaments came to Whippoorwill at the end of the summer, I and my fellow serious caddie/players would be assigned to the premier competitors—Jerry Courville (father and son), Bob Gardner, Willie Turnesa. We studied them even more intensely. These were not fat white guys wearing plaid pants. They were world-class athletes, only a hair shy of pro-tour level. They could work magic with a golf ball.

To assist someone at that level, particularly when you have barely entered puberty, leaves you no choice but to expand your imagination. From a hundred and eighty yards out on a chilly, wet morning, with the wind quartering out of the right and your player facing an all-carry shot over a bunker with a drop-dead fall-off beyond the green and a putt that has to come in from below the hole, meaning the shot-in must land short and right of the pin and hold smack there… what options do you hold ready to give your guy if he asks? Remember, your player is so good he can do virtually anything with the ball—flight it high or low, with left or right spin, take ten yards off or put ten yards on. Not to mention you have to know the yardage down to the foot. Without yardage books or markers. All by eyeball.

As for working on our own games, since my brother caddies and I were aspiring players, the only time we could get on the golf course was Monday—Caddies' Day, when the club was closed to everybody but us. We routinely played fifty-four holes, three times around. We'd get to the first tee so early, in darkness so deep, that one of us would have to crouch directly behind our buddies as they teed off. That way we could glimpse the first ten feet of the ball's flight and be able to guess where it would land. One Monday we played seventy-two holes. Four rounds.

Love of the game.

In January, you could find me beside the Sawmill River Parkway in the only space in town broad and long enough to hit a full five-iron, practicing until the last atom of daylight. The ground was frozen solid as steel. My clubhead rang off it with a sound like a bell. Balls were so dead with the cold it was like hitting stones.

That's how I feel now, here in California, in my little house behind the big house. I have my list of approved players—Dostoevsky, Tolstoy, Hemingway, Mark Twain, Virginia Woolf, Melville, Faulkner, Fitzgerald, Chekhov, Harper Lee, Philip Roth, Saul Bellow, Homer, Plato, Xenophon, Shakespeare, King David.

I'm not motivated by greed, fame, or recognition. I'm in it for the game itself. Ambition, yes. I want to be good. Like myself at thirteen, I can't hit the ball for shit. I can't make it go right or left, I can't hit it as long as I want, and I sure as hell can't do it on demand. So I do it over and over, and when I'm done I do it over again.

I do it in all weathers. And when I'm too tired to keep doing it myself, I watch other players whose level of skill I aspire to. I watch them do it.

All I know how to do is work.

41. WRITING SHIT

When I describe my writing work in this era, I'm being hard on myself. My stuff isn't as bad as that. It's bad, don't get me wrong. Far below the threshold of publication. But its heart is in the right place.

I'm trying. I'm giving it my all. The thought of tailoring my output to any market or to please any imagined audience never enters my mind. This is for me. I 'm writing to save my own life.

Some days I do nothing but copy other writers. Hemingway. Henry Miller. These are the masters whose styles I love, whose fluency and authenticity I want for my own work.

I sit at my table with *The Sun Also Rises* open and Mo snoozing beside the typewriter.

> I put on a bathrobe and slippers and went to the door.
> It was Brett. Back of her was the count. He was holding
> a great bunch of roses.

I type that. I type the whole chapter and the one after that and the one after that. Do I have a plan? Am I taking notes? I'm working mindlessly, like a chimpanzee. I want Hemingway's stuff to sink into me by osmosis.

But I'm paying attention too. Hemingway's style is cinematic. He makes you see.

> I went to the door. It was Brett. Back of her was
> the count.

I'm trying to copy that. When you haul yourself up into the cab of a tractor-trailer, where does your foot go? What grab-handle do you seize? With which hand? Is the metal cold? What do you see as you slide into the driver's seat? Smell? Hear? What does the instrument panel look like? What do you see through the windshield? What emotions are you feeling? Are you excited? Scared? Bored? Do you hate being here? Do you love it? What does it mean to you? How can I, the writer, reproduce that in you, the reader?

I copy Henry Miller for his passion and for the balls-out guts to tell us, his readers, what the fuck is what.

> Once you have given up the ghost, everything follows with dead certainty, even in the midst of chaos. From the beginning it was never anything but chaos: it was a fluid which enveloped me, which I breathed in through the gills. In everything I quickly saw the opposite, the contradiction, and between the real and the unreal the irony, the paradox. I was my own worst enemy. There was nothing I wished to do which I could just as well not do. Even as a child, when I lacked for nothing, I wanted to die: I felt that nothing would be proved, substantiated, added or subtracted by continuing an existence which I had not asked for. Everybody around me was a failure, or if not a failure, ridiculous. I never helped anyone expecting that it would do me any good; I helped because I was helpless to do otherwise. To want to change the condition of affairs seemed futile to me; nothing would be altered, I was convinced, except by a change of heart, and who could change the hearts of men? Now and then a friend was

converted: it was something to make me puke. I had no more need of God than He had of me, and if there were one, I often said to myself, I would meet Him calmly and spit in His face.

That's writing. That's what I want to do.

SIDEBAR: THE FREAK LIFE # 1

THE MOST ALL-IN, burn-the-boats freaks I ever saw were at Buster Holmes' in the French Quarter.

Buster Holmes' is an eatery at the corner of Burgundy and Orleans. It's still there, though in a whole other gentrified incarnation.

When I was there you could get a plate of beans and rice, I mean a big honking wad ladled straight out of a twenty-gallon cook pot, with a huge chunk of baguette and a slab of butter on the side for twenty-seven cents. I'm not making this up. A Coke cost twenty-five cents.

Buster's was divided into two sections. The upscale half was for black people, locals from the quarter, friends of Buster's. The down-market side was for hippies. No one transgressed. You ate at a horseshoe-shaped counter or, if you got there early enough, at one of the tables along the walls.

The faces on the locals were worthy of Avedon or Helmut Newton. But what I remember is the freaks. There's no way to describe them in prose. Have you seen Edward Curtis' photos of Native American warriors and women from the 1800s? The skin. The eyes. That's what these road hippies looked like. The men had hair down to their asses. The women looked like Dorothea Lange's photos from the Dust Bowl. I ate at Buster's night after night and never raised the nerve to say a peep to any of them.

It seems preposterous and even ridiculously naïve in today's world, but at that time there was the sense—and many people believed this with all their hearts—that the world was changing. The old predatory ways had been superseded. A new culture and ethic were being born.

But these burnt-black, flowing-maned road hippies were not seeking to overthrow an existing order. They had left that order behind. They were living their own new order.

Ask me if I've ever had a hero. I'll tell you, "Them."

SIDEBAR: THE FREAK LIFE #2

I WAS IN GRIFFITH Park at some kind of hippie political event. John Trudell, the Native American poet and activist (1946–2015), was speaking. I didn't know who he was. But he radiated a charisma that was irresistible.

"You see these guys at the back of the crowd, the ones in the suits with the dark glasses?" Trudell pointed out a pair of serious-looking white men observing from the margins.

"These are FBI agents. They follow me everywhere. They think I'm a revolutionary Communist, conspiring to overthrow the government. Lemme tell you what I think about that."

Sure enough, the two men monitoring the gathering looked like feds. They had the short haircuts, the emotionless expressions, the suits and white shirts, the lace-up shoes.

"To me, capitalism and communism are the same thing. There's no daylight between them. I see no difference between Russia and America. Both are systems of extraction and exploitation—extraction of resources from the Earth and exploitation of labor from the tyrannized and the benighted.

"Both systems are controlled by a small, secretive cabal whose aim is the perpetuation of its own wealth and power. Both systems exploit their people and imprison their minds with lies and propaganda. Both despoil the Earth. Both believe that this planet belongs to man and that man has the right to rape anything he calls his own.

"I come from the opposite belief system. To me, the Earth is our mother. She does not belong to us. We belong to her. Our role is to protect her so she may care for us."

Again, John Trudell indicated the federal agents.

"So these guys have got me right on one count. I am their enemy. I hate everything they stand for, and I will work every day of my life and give my life, if I have to, to see it all brought down. But they're wrong about me being a communist. To me, that system and ours in America are one and the same."

Ask me if I have another hero. I'll say, "Him

SIDEBAR: THE FREAK LIFE #3

WHEN I LEFT TINSLEY Oilfield Maintenance in Buras, Louisiana, (don't try to follow the chronology; even I can't remember it), I drove back to San Francisco. I was hoping against hope that Lesley would take me back.

I got to her place in the Avenues around one in the afternoon after a six-day crossing. Lesley wasn't home. She was at work. I forget what job she had. Her boyfriend was home. I had never met him. I didn't know she had a boyfriend. It was hard to stop myself from imagining him on top of her or her on top of him.

He and I, in a state of excruciating awkwardness, took a walk down to the beach, waiting for Lesley to get home. He was a good guy, a long-haired hippie. I forget his name, except that he was from Kentucky and had come out to San Francisco about two years earlier.

Finally Lesley got home. I can't remember anything she said or I said, except that the conversation took place in her kitchen. She was cutting up a chicken and spooning Crisco into a black cast-iron skillet. She invited me to stay for dinner. I couldn't do it. It was four flights of stairs back down to the street. I climbed back into the van and headed down the coast to a house where my Marine friends Charles and David lived with a band of long-haired freaks.

When you enlist in a cult or a subculture—whether it's religious, political, or utopian—you receive indoctrination. Members initiate you. It could be the Communist Party in Moscow circa 1918. It could be a kibbutz in Mandate Palestine. It could be the Marine Corps. People teach you.

You change.

You want to change.

You shed one style of clothing and don another. You acquire certain insignia or artifacts. Your new friends give them to you. These are threshold totems—talismans of initiation. You apply alterations to your physical body. Maybe your head gets shaved, maybe you grow your hair long. You get tattooed, or you have tattoos effaced. Parts of your body may get trimmed off.

In all these transfigurations you are a willing and eager participant. I know I was. My hair couldn't grow fast enough to satisfy me.

Entering a cult, you undergo prescribed initiatory experiences. These are exclusionary in the sense that "normal" or "straight" people have not or will not engage in them. Maybe they've never even heard of them. In these experiences, sometimes chemically induced, other times brought on by some form of physical or mental privation—cold, heat, exhaustion, exposure to something theatrical and disorienting—you see things you've never seen before, particularly about yourself.

A world is opened to you, a universe founded upon novel assumptions, following laws that are entirely different—if not the direct inverse—of the precepts you had always, until then, believed to be true.

You embrace these new norms, these assumptions. You swear

allegiance to them. You thank God that fate or luck has brought you to this place. You want to learn these laws. You embrace the posture of an aspirant, an acolyte, a renunciant.

To formalize your inclusion in this new community, you must perform some ceremonial act. This is an initiatory rite, a ritual crossing of a threshold. By its completion, you repudiate permanently any chance of re-integration into the world you left behind. Maybe you are required to commit a crime. Maybe you undergo a hallucinatory or even psychotic episode of self-annihilation. Maybe you are asked to renounce something or someone, publicly and with finality.

You learn a new language in a cult. Slang. Jargon. Secret terms that the Man, Mister Charley, does not know and cannot penetrate. You and your new friends may be standing six inches from an enforcer of the greater society's norms; yet you can carry on a conversation of sedition or contempt and he won't understand a word. This new language possesses power. By its employment you identify other initiates, and they recognize you. Your rhythm of speech changes. You acquire new hand gestures. Your posture alters. Subcultures from which you may have formerly been excluded now open their portals to you. You enter eagerly. You never want to leave.

Certain texts are scripture in each new age. These tomes are placed into your hands with reverence. You accept them in the sacramental spirit. *The Tao de Ching*, the *I Ching*, *The Way of Zen* by Alan Watts. *Stranger in a Strange Land* by Robert Heinlein, *Dune* by Frank Herbert. *Damien* and *Siddhartha* by Hermann Hesse. *Meetings with Remarkable Men* by G.I. Gurdjieff. *In Search of the Miraculous* by P.D. Ouspensky, along with *The Fourth Way* and *Tertium Organum. Sartor Resartus* by Thomas Carlyle.

I read R.D. Laing, I read Victor Frankl. Anything by Ken Kesey or Peter Matthiessen, Gary Snyder, Jack Kerouac, Alan Ginsberg, R. Crumb, Bob Dylan. These sacred texts are passed from one hand to another like relics of a religious past or harbingers of a new faith. "Here, brother. Read this."

Poetry.

Music.

Drugs.

Sex.

I'm the only one in the hippie house who is not getting laid. The issue is moot for me. I can't even think about women. The only thing I want is to exorcise and eradicate from my psyche every belief, assumption, thought, aspiration, dream, hope and moral principle I have been taught or imbibed in my entire life. They don't work. They have led me to this. I hate them. I abhor every person and institution that has brainwashed or indoctrinated me into believing them. I hate myself for buying into this bullshit. I want to replace it all as fast and as permanently as I can with whatever long-haired, counter-culture, freakazoid Mr. Natural doctrine and belief system I can derive from my new friends in the house and from Charles and David.

I want to be like the freaks I saw at Buster Holmes' in the French Quarter. Can I pass through a membrane that will deposit me, somehow, on the other side? I want it. I want to find that portal and transmigrate through. Does there exist a state of mind, a mode of being, a sphere of consciousness that will somehow obliterate everything I have ever believed? I want to find this and jump through with both feet.

In the meantime, I have to find work.

I get on as the hippie janitor at a gourmet restaurant in the nearby seaside village. My salary is forty-five dollars a week, plus a free lunch. I show up at six in the morning. No one is there but me. I park my van in the slot stenciled ERWIN for the owner. My job is to clean up the joint so it's spotless when the chef and the kitchen staff arrive at ten-thirty.

The restaurant is owned by a handsome German couple, Heidi and Erwin Kaminski. Framed photos on the wall show them presiding over prior establishments in Gstaad, Baden-Baden, and Lake Constance. The restaurant is a no-shit, Euro-apex operation. On consecutive lines in the visitors' book reside the following signatures:

Ringo Starr
John Lennon
George Harrison
Paul McCartney

My first task each morning is to line the garbage cans. Erwin shows me exactly how he wants it done. I am to take newspaper and, starting with a triple layer at the bottom, spiral upward along the flanks of the cans to the rim, concluding the operation with a neat, hospital-type fold at the top. The only problem is each morning as I'm cantilevered forward with my head deep in the cylinder of the garbage can, I find myself caught up in the articles in the newspaper. I'm reading them. I lose track of time. Ten minutes later I have torqued myself into an upside-down corkscrew trying to find page three of an article I had started reading on the front page.

By noon I have swept and scoured every surface in the establishment, including the underside of the griddle and the linoleum surfaces behind the toilet seats in the ladies' room, not to mention steam-cleaning and flushing out the grease traps, vacuuming the carpets, replacing the toilet paper (with a V-fold in the center of the topmost strip) and hand towels in both bathrooms, restocking the tampons in the coin-deposit dispenser in the distaff loo and the Trojan-Enz prophylactics in the gentlemen's, polishing the mirrors, double-Lysoling the sinks, Windexing the street and interior-facing windows (using newspaper not paper towels, per

Erwin, as drying instruments) as well as the mirror surfaces throughout the restaurant and buffing the brass picture frames and doorknobs until you can see your face in them, or rather until Erwin can see his.

From the restaurant I head to the garden. A counterculture-friendly homeowner has made available an unused two-acre plot to any commune or aggregation of long-hairs that wishes to grow its own organic produce. Our house takes over the lower quarter. Somehow I become the farmer. Everyone else has gotten bored after the first week. I drive straight over from the restaurant. A young hippie lives in the garden. His name is Jeremy. He's sixteen years old from Paducah, Kentucky. He has no car, no driver's license, no draft card, no money. We become instant friends.

Jeremy lives on honey, nuts, and raw vegetables from the garden. He is not associated with our house or with any of the other communal bastions who are cultivating other gardens in this donated plot. He just lives here. Jeremy chants, he prays, he meditates, he hikes in the hills. His eyes are as cornflower-blue as Van Gogh's, his face and torso sun-browned as wheat toast. Jeremy reads. Every day when I get there, he has another book for me. All are Byzantinely obscure and absolutely fascinating. My favorites are a set of brown-paper pamphlets, each approximately twenty pages, hand-typed and hand-pressed, and attributed to Prof. Dr. Edmund Boudreau Szekely.

I have never heard of Prof. Dr. Szekely but his stuff is mesmerizing. The pamphlets are about trees. How trees talk to each other, how they survive heat and cold, how they process sunlight via photosynthesis, how they produce sugar and energy from sunlight, enabling even oaks and American elms a hundred feet tall to suck up nutrition from the soil and deliver it to the highest leaves on the loftiest branch of the organism.

"The human race receives nothing but blessings from trees," says Jeremy. "Think about it. They produce fruit for us, and nuts, olives, pomegranates, you name it. They provide shade in the summer and serve as windbreaks in the winter. A tree can't move. It can't hurt you. Trees hold the soil. They stabilize the water table. They even sacrifice their limbs and trunks for us in the form of firewood. They never hurt us. They give and give. And they're beautiful."

The season passes. I'm planting winter vegetables now. Although I have progressed dutifully and enthusiastically through the stages of hippie initiation, I confess I have never felt entirely at ease in the communal homestead. I'm happier with Jeremy or just by myself in the garden. I come home each day with armloads of butter lettuce or beets or carrots, but my compatriots somehow prefer produce from Safeway.

43. SELF-DISCIPLINE

I have one other friend beside Jeremy. He's still my friend today. His name is Tony Keppelman. I met him at the second house our communal band moved into. The house is called Rancho Grande, although it's not a rancho and is far from grande. It's in a place called Hitchcock Canyon, which is as gorgeous as it sounds. Next door to this house, physically abutting it, is a charming rustic cabin.

A girl named Cody lives there, with her little son Joel.

In any community of like-aspiring individuals, no matter how diffuse or geographically dispersed, one female will stand out as the queen. Maybe she's the prettiest, maybe the most accomplished or the one with the most social seniority. Maybe she's just the most charismatic. Cody is all these, plus she possesses the ultimate street cred of having taken, so local lore maintains, over five hundred acid trips. If you think that's nothing, start with five and see how far you get.

Tony is Cody's boyfriend.

We become friends instantly. I simply gravitate to him. Tony is the first person I've ever met who actually possesses self-discipline.

I have never encountered this before.

Other individuals I've admired for their focus and commitment have jobs or are in the military. They adhere to their institution's norms and protocols. That's discipline, but it's not self-discipline. It's externally imposed, not generated from within.

Tony is just a young man alone—self-motivated, self-validated, self-reinforced.

I study Tony as if he were an avatar from another star system. He lives in a house he designed and built himself. Everything in it is original and unique. Tony has invented a fireplace fabricated of nothing but a metal flue, loose bricks, and steel L-bars. The thing probably costs four bucks total, but it draws powerfully even in the wind, heats the entire interior in seconds, and can be dismantled in five minutes and taken away to be reassembled in the next house.

Tony is a photographer. He has worked for Ansel Adams. He has been an assistant to Edward Weston. He has built darkrooms for them. For himself, Tony has crafted a developing suite with self-sloshing trays and all kinds of other zany but fascinating features. Tony's heritage is Swiss. He's a born inventor. He builds his own bank of synthesizers to play his own brand of music. He's a near-concert level keyboard player. He plays classical guitar. The fingernails of his right hand are like iron. You could strike a match off the callouses on the fingertips of his left.

Auto mechanics? Tony can diagnose and repair anything automotive. With me assisting, he takes the transmission out of his Ford pickup, using a dolly lift he designed himself, replaces the synchronizers and puts the whole thing back together and back into the truck. The operation would have cost five hundred dollars at the dealership or a repair facility, if they could even be trusted to do it. Tony bangs it out for twenty-six bucks. He's also a finish carpenter. That's how he earns his living when he's not working in the darkroom. He can design and build cabinets, tables, chairs. He can craft a barn-style beam ceiling. If you can draw it, Tony can fabricate it. Tony doesn't buy shoes, he makes them. Want a leather jacket? He'll sketch it and cut and dye it and put it on your shoulders. He has made guitars. He has made a theorbo. He's a great organic cook. He runs marathons.

I never saw anyone organize a day like Tony. He's awake and in action at four-thirty. He runs. He does yoga. He'll make a breakfast of fresh veggies and eggs straight from under the laying hen. Then he sits down at the piano—the solitary item in his house that he hasn't built himself.

For ninety minutes Tony does scales and exercises. His focus is total. For the next hour he plays Bach or Chopin or some other classical piece I've never heard of but that he beats his brains out trying to get right or get better than he played it the last time. Later in the day he'll work on his fingering for the guitar, sitting upright in impeccable posture with the instrument on one knee at an angle like Segovia. Tony holds to his schedule like a monk. Cody will try to get Tony to come over in the afternoon so she can fuck him. He won't go. He has work to do.

Tony is moral. He has ethics. He lives by a code. A lot of weird, self-infatuated shit goes down inevitably in any counterculture environment. Tony won't stand for it. He gets up and leaves. And he doesn't come back.

In the end, he and Cody part ways. Tony can't abide some of the stuff she's doing or the ways she treats people. He's not too keen on my friends either.

"Why are you living with these people?" he asks me one day.

I don't have an answer.

44. THE MAN COMES AROUND

Eleven months into my sojourn in Hitchcock Canyon, representatives of the active-duty Marine Corps appear—a Gunnery Sergeant and a Staff Sergeant in uniform. They're looking for Charles. He has decamped to Guadalajara. His hair is down to his shoulders. David? He's working in a uranium mine in Grants, New Mexico. No one in the house gives up anything about them.

Somehow, I am not on the Marine Corps' radar. Yet.

I wind up smoking a Marlboro with the staff sergeant out in the driveway. He's a Pace College economics major from Hartsdale, New York, a few miles from my original reserve unit—a three-tour veteran 0311 (infantry) of Vietnam with a Bronze Star and two Purple Hearts.

I ask him how hard the Marine Corps will search for Charles and David and what fate awaits the two of them, if and when they get caught.

The sergeant shakes his head. "Marines these days," he says, "even decorated regulars are smoking dope, dropping acid, flashing peace signs, and getting FUCK THE CORPS tattoos. You think the Commandant wants that on the six o'clock news?

"The Corps doesn't really want to catch up with your friends. What the hell are we gonna do with them? It's a black eye for us, any way you look at it."

The communal house starts breaking up. At its peak, the bedrooms and couches slept twelve people, seven guys and five girls. Now it's down to eight. One couple moves north to Berkeley. Another packs up and heads home to Brooklyn.

Me?

I'm pretty through with it too.

45. KINGS OF THE ROAD

Late in the season, when the Deliciouses are done, the crews move on to the Winesaps. These are small, hard apples used primarily for cooking or cider. They have a particularly nasty stem. It's cold now. There's frost on the fruit early in the morning. You must leave the stem on each apple. That means your thumb and forefinger get sliced over and over.

I ask John, "How do you pick Winesaps?"

"With a great deal of pain."

Practically everyone now is walking wounded. The road—I mean the real road, the road these fruit tramps live on—is a dangerous place. Guys get beaten up, slashed by knives, run over by cars in the dark. Other tramps steal their bedrolls. They steal their shoes. Cops work them over or just hassle them for fun. They pass out on benches when the night drops below freezing.

Yet there's a hardcore wisdom to the choice these gentlemen have made, even though for most of them it may never have been a choice at all. These itinerant workers have made their home in a universe from which the rest of us have spent the bulk of our lives fleeing. This is John's world, and Clayton's and Marvin's.

If the economy goes into the tank tomorrow, John will be fine. Alien invasion? No problem. I admire these guys. They remind me of the road hippies from Buster Holmes' in the French Quarter. They don't fear "the worst that might happen." They're living it right now, and they can hack it. They can travel anywhere in the country without owning a car, find work without a résumé, scare up dinner without a dime in their pockets, and get in out of the rain without renting or owning.

How do tramps die?

"Trains kill 'em. That's one," says John.

YOU MUST BE TERRIFIC TO RIDE THE UNION PACIFIC

"Electrocution's another. Guys collect copper, to sell. They'll throw a rope or a chain over a power line and pull it down. Alcohol of course will waste you. Fall down a stairway. Pick a fight with a guy with a knife. And drowning. A sleep-camp is always best beside a river. Step wrong at night and you're in the drink."

Half the pickers now are from the Wenatchee jail. Deputies drive them to the orchard each morning in busses with bars on the windows. Once the inmates get their breakfast, they melt away. Their ladders wait, flat on the ground. You find their sacks under the trees. I ask a deputy why he doesn't chase them.

"They'll be back in jail by tonight. They're walking there now. Where else they gonna go?"

46. MARVIN MOUNTAIN

Late October now. Nine-tenths of the orchard has been picked bare. Two weeks to End of Season. Guys are pulling the pin now in numbers. Ivan from Tacoma vanishes first. We wake up one morning and he's gone. Then Teddy from Kentucky. Then Big Mike from Seattle and a day later Little Mike.

"Don't even think about it," says John to me.

Clayton from Oklahoma disappears next. "Damn fool," says John. "Ten days from his bonus."

Our table is down to John, me, and Marvin. Marvin accepts us. We're the only ones who don't call him Chief.

My picking technique has progressed painfully. I can get two apples with my right hand now but still only one with my left. These Winesaps are killers. No one even jokes about them. We pick and eat and sleep and get up and do it again. Nights are bitter. Blankets from guys who've pulled the pin get doubled up and even tripled.

Two nights into November, Marvin hemorrhages. He lurches out of his bunk at two in the morning, banging in the dark into the table where he stacks his clothes, and crashes like a bomb onto the floor. John hits the lights. Marvin's habit is to sleep naked. Blood paints the insides of his thighs.

"I'm bleeding from the ass!" our friend cries.

John and I rush him into town. I'm driving. John is wedging wadded-up newspaper into the crack of Marvin's butt. The Urgent Care is shuttered. It takes us half an hour to find the hospital emergency room, guided by a cop we flag down at Dixie Donuts. John clearly has stanched bleeding wounds before. He strips his own T-shirt, working it between

Marvin's cheeks and pressing it hard against the rupture.

I've witnessed this type of bleeding myself when I worked for Dr. Jeff in North Carolina. Marvin lies sideways on the mattress in the back of the van. "Sorry, man, I'm bleeding all over your shit."

John gives me a look over the top of Marvin's skull.

The emergency room takes forty-five minutes to wheel Marvin through the double doors for treatment. It's an hour shy of dawn before the hospital finishes with John and me, after we have filled out what feels like twenty pages of "indigent intake" forms. Neither of us knows Marvin's last name. Breakfast is milk in half-pint cartons and hard-boiled eggs in the hospital commissary.

John refuses to return to the orchard till he knows Marvin's fate. I'm thinking we'll lose the day. We'll blow our bonuses.

Sometime before noon a nurse finds us to tell us Marvin has expired. That's the word she uses. "When?" John asks.

"Six hours ago."

"We been sitting here that whole fucking time."

John insists on staying until someone in Records or Administration finds Marvin's people. He won't let the hospital dump the body. But the social worker has three other John Does just this night. I can't reach Boros, our supervisor, by phone so I drive back to the orchard by myself and track him down under the trees. The family name Payroll has for Marvin is "Mountain."

"Indians all go by aliases."

I pick up John at two. We're back to the orchard by three, ready to get in what hours we can before sunset. Boros won't let us. He's docking us both our season bonuses.

I've never seen John get angry before. No veins stick out on his neck. His voice barely changes. But he threatens to go to the Wenatchee newspaper or to the governor himself about sanitary conditions at the orchard, including the showers, the rats, and the charred mattresses out back. "And when I'm done," he tells Boros, "I'll come looking for you."

I'd like to say this did some good. It didn't. Appearing at the hospital the next evening, John and I are told that Marvin's corpse has been designated for "A.D."

"What the hell's that?"

The admin girl won't tell us.

It takes John half-climbing through the counter window before she acknowledges, "Administrative disposal."

"What does that mean? We're his friends. We want to be there."

"I'm sorry. Disposal of the remains has already taken place."

Six days to go. The last Winesaps are being thinned from the trees. Only pockets remain. Bunkhouses are so empty now the orchard adds a second bonus. Two bucks extra for every bin you pick between now and season's end.

In the chow hall, we're getting seconds on desserts and cookies. The hands are so few, the cooks haven't figured out how to plan their cutbacks.

Boros has decided to restore John's bonus and mine. John's is 571 bins with four days to go. My total for seven weeks is 157. I'm happy. A hundred and fifty-seven dollars is enough to get the vacuum advance on my engine fixed and maybe pay for a couple of retreads. Above and beyond the five hundred bucks I've stashed from regular pay.

More than enough to finish the book.

Still, every cell in my body is crying out, "Pull the pin! Pull the pin!"

Two a.m., three nights from the finish, I'm tiptoeing across the creaking bunkhouse floor.

"Where you think you're going?" It's John's voice in the darkness.

"To my van to get a smoke."

I hear his Zippo strike and see the flare as he lights one of his own Camels and holds it out to me.

We make it.

Bonus checks. Final breakfast. From the cooks "for the road": homemade oatmeal raisin cookies wrapped in wax paper.

Winter has reached these high Washington latitudes. Frost crystals on the grass. Ice-skim on the puddles. Limbs in the orchards are bare. I give John a ride into Wenatchee, where his sister-in-law is coming from Seattle to pick him up. He will rest for a few days before heading south. We shake hands beside the ball field where we first met.

Another tramp named Jerry chances by. "Going for the oranges?" he asks me, meaning the season starting in a week around Mesa, Arizona.

"Nah," I say. "Gotta get back to work."

Book Four

BARTHOLD FLES

I've heard that birds sing out of pure joy. I don't believe it. I don't believe writers write or painters paint because they're bursting with the exuberance of life. They write because they're in pain. They write to exorcise that pain. They write or paint because if they didn't, the pain would kill them or drive them mad.

What is that pain? Is it specific? Is it really the love you lost or the child who drowned or the friend who burned to death in a Humvee when you were two feet away and couldn't save him?

I don't think so.

In the hippie garden, Jeremy and I used to ponder the concept of the *bodhisattva*, the soul who has achieved personal salvation and is approved for paradise but elects to come back. The bodhisattva signs up for another life, not for himself or herself, but to help others.

Can there be an act loftier or nobler in the human or post-human sphere?

But what does that say about the sphere itself? It's hell. That's what it says. Otherwise, why would coming back be an act worthy of beatification?

You and I read something on the page and it strikes us to the core. Maybe it's Tolstoy, maybe Toni Morrison. We think, *My God, that is so true! It's so real.*

It isn't. It's art. Art is artifice.

Soldiers come back from war and write about the agony they inflicted or endured. Other men and women at home, riven by heartbreak, write blues songs or produce movies—maybe even rollicking farces and comedies—to make the pain stop.

But what happens when you try to write it straight, to tell the tale exactly as it happened? What happens is you realize you've "forgotten" it. You can't access the emotion. The pain is too much for the heart to bear.

This is not real forgetting, as in some memory that has slipped away. It's emotional amnesia. It's selective self-anesthesia. It's forgetting for self-protection.

Or let's say you remember events perfectly. You still can't write them straight-up. If you did, you would overwhelm the reader. Your depiction would come off like the ravings of a lunatic or the inarticulate cries produced in the moment of actual agony.

Seeking to access such moments as an artist, you have to go to the place you go when you write fiction. You have to reframe the event. You have to apply distance. You have to reinvent it. You have to make it up.

The only way the singer can express this pain is as an artist, meaning she has to find a mental and emotional place at one remove (or more) from the straight event–and then perform the event.

When Edith Piaf sings a *chanson* she has written of the pain of love, she is acting. She is performing. She is not experiencing the actual pain as she might have in the moment, assuming the song comes from a real event that she really experienced. If she had tried to do this, she would not be able to sing at all. So she goes to the place where an actor goes, or a performer, and produces, because she is an artist, a brilliant simulacrum of that pain.

And this expression of pain becomes a gift to every heart who hears it. Women and men in the audience weep. They are recalling a pain that is not Edith's but is the same as Edith's, their version of the pain Edith is expressing in her rendition of the song.

The music is art.

The lyrics are art.

The performance is art.

The pain expressed is derived from real pain. Its genesis is actual suffering, endured by a real person. But the song itself and its rendition are not the *real* pain, or the artist would choke up and break down. Instead the warble in her voice, the catching of the throat in her performance is *art*. It is not life. It is artifice.

There's something very deep here. How do we endure pain? How do we transcend it?

We turn it into art.

We emerge from prison bearing agonies that would crush a stone. How do we survive these? We transform them. We get a tattoo. We ink an entire sleeve. We cover our chest and back with swastikas, death's-heads, and quotes in bogus Mandarin from *Kill Bill, Volume Two*. We blast our pecs. We pierce our flesh. We customize Harleys. We shave our skull. We craft an image of ourselves, even if it's one—especially if it's one—as predictable as low-ride jeans and chrome-link wallet chains.

That's art. That's our novel.

This is what the writer wrestles with. This is the passage. You pound keyboards until you wear the sonsofbitches out. Each page is trash. Unreadable. Unpublishable.

You're stuck. You're immured within the pain. It doesn't matter if your pain is frivolous or unworthy. It doesn't matter if it's not the exalted anguish of Abelard and Heloise or Dante and Beatrice or Aleksandr Solzhenitsyn in the gulag. It's your pain. It's real. Your ordeal of expression is as valid as Shakespeare's, or Milton's, or Virginia Woolf's.

That's what I'm trying to do. Sitting for months at my manual Smith-Corona, seeking the idiom, the phrasing, the tone of voice, that will let me express that agony that is eating my guts like cancer.

I never do. As Joni Mitchell wrote (I'm paraphrasing) ...

> He tried but he could not get it down.
> Not for truth or mystery.
> Not for love or money.

Yet, one day, I was able to write. One day I *could* produce a page that was more than an inarticulate grunt.

One day I could write a page that was a story.

What we do as artists, you and I, is in its way as lofty an enterprise as that undertaken by God Himself when He made this world. We powerless, broken mortals, blind and deaf and stumbling, afflicting one another and destroying ourselves, the best parts of ourselves, in isolation, fearful of and furious at our brothers and sisters... yet somehow we find within ourselves the capacity to produce that which heals others, which brings balm and surcease of pain, even if only for a few moments in the lamplit dimness of a cabaret, to men and women we don't know and never will.

We are artists now.

We are performers.

We are artificers.

What has been lost? The pain is lost. That's the point. We have, in a way, become monsters, in that our pain, a certain rendition of it anyway, can no longer reach us. But we have become angels too, or better yet, true humans.

Nine weeks after I get back from Washington State, I finish the book about Burton Lines. I call it *Bethesda Transfer*, my fictional name for the trucking company where I worked for Hugh Reaves and pulled the pin. Here's what I wrote in *The War of Art*.

> I never did find a buyer for the book. Or the next one, either.
>
> It was ten more years before I got the first check for something I had written and ten more after that before a novel, *The Legend of Bagger Vance*, was actually published. But that moment when I first hit the keys to type out THE END was epochal. I remember rolling the last page out and adding it to the stack that was the finished manuscript.
>
> Nobody knew I was done. Nobody cared. But I knew. I felt like a dragon I'd been battling all my life had just dropped dead at my feet and gasped out its last sulfuric breath.
>
> Rest in peace, motherfucker.

The next morning I went over to Paul's camper for coffee and told him I had finished. "Good for you," he said without looking up. "Start the next one today."

49. ART IS ARTIFICE #2

From California, Mo and I drive back to New York. I'm now thirty-four years old, twelve years into the writing—or running away from writing—life. The following excerpt is from *The Knowledge* (2016). "Teaspoon" is my fictional name for Mo.

> My apartment is a few blocks north of Nicolette's, on Fifteenth between Eighth and Ninth. I have two rooms compared to her one. The front room is my bed, a kitchenette, and, amazingly, a working fireplace. The back room is a table and chair with my typewriter. The reason I picked this apartment is because it's on the third floor, with an external staircase that runs two flights down straight into the rear courtyard. The open area between the buildings on Fifteenth and Fourteenth is as wide as and longer than a football field. It runs the whole length of the block. The dining terrace of a Portuguese restaurant sits right across the way beneath my window, with a Chinese takeout next door and all kinds of interesting stuff going on after dark.
>
> I took the apartment for my cat, Teaspoon. Teaspoon is an outdoor cat. I didn't want to imprison him indoors just because we had moved to New York. I cut a cat-sized hole in a piece of plywood and stuck it in the window frame in the back room right above the external staircase. In summer I leave the hole open for Teaspoon to come and go. In the winter I stuff an old sweater into the hole

for insulation. Teaspoon tugs the sweater out with one paw when he wants to go outside. It's not too efficient heat-wise, but it's low-tech and it works.

My friend Jake is always telling me to get rid of Teaspoon.

"Stretch, you gotta lose that cat."

He repeats this every time I see him.

"A single guy with a cat. It doesn't look right."

There's no way I'm gonna get rid of Teaspoon, single guy or not. He's the only person who gives a damn about me and who I myself care about. I found him when he was a tiny kitten... [He] has been with me through many, many changes, as they say on the West Coast, and has always been true blue. He's the kind of cat who would lend you money, no questions asked, if he had it.

This is my life in New York City, post-Burton Lines, post-Beebe Orchards, post-*Bethesda Transfer*. I drive a cab. I scratch out freelance gigs as a copywriter.

After six months I find an actual job. I have a cubicle now at Ted Bates, an ad agency in Times Square. I have friends. I'm dating women. But basically I'm holed up in my back room, pounding the keys.

Mo and I have become two halves of the same being. He lives the cat life. I live the writer life. You know how they say wild animals exist totally in the present? That's me too. I still can't write worth a damn. If I succeed in hammering out a decent declarative sentence, it's because I sat there all afternoon composing it six ways to Palm Fucking Sunday. That, or I worked myself into a writing trance and just let it come out of me uncensored and un-self-consciously.

I have a real Muse. The goddess, I mean. But Mo is my muse too. He's the reincarnation of the redheaded cat that used to visit me when I lived in the woods in North Carolina.

I admire Mo. He lives the life he was born to live. It never occurs to him—and never could occur—to do anything else. When he's unhappy, he lets you know. When times are good, he lets you know too. He's self-sufficient. I feed him, yeah, but the act is entirely superfluous. He scrounges pizza crusts and fish heads and heaven knows what else from the restaurant kitchens in the intra-building space below my window.

My cat has his world outside the window, down the staircase. His world is full of hazards, ordeals, characters, and adventures. Other cats, the pizza guy, the lady manager from the Szechuan restaurant, not to mention dogs, rats, pigeons, cockroaches, plus who knows what other personalities, humanoid and otherwise, he runs into crossing Abingdon Square and Eighth Avenue on his way to Nicolette's basement apartment.

I have my world too. It's full of characters just like Mo's. My cat doesn't talk about his characters, and I don't talk about mine.

I enter my world just like Mo enters his. He scrunches down and slips through the porthole in the window above the fire escape. I enter a portal too. I wish I could say mine opens onto a magical land where inspiration flows and I enter "the zone" of creative inspiration. Mostly it's blue-collar hell. I'm trying to craft a story when I have no idea what a story is. I stare at a sentence and ask myself, "Why the fuck did I write this? What is it supposed to mean?" From *The Knowledge*:

> One thing you learn though, if you're a writer, is that nobody gives a damn about you or your work. My friend Jake will ask me, "How's the book going?" and it's all over his face that he couldn't give less of a shit. If anything, he's hoping I'll fail. When I report any

setback, I can see him fighting to keep from grinning.

My uncle Charlie's the same, even though he loves me like a son. "Still writing those books?" he'll ask, in the same tone he'd use to say, "Still squeegee-ing windshields at the entrance to the Midtown Tunnel?"

Have you seen *Taxi Driver*? There's a moment when the protagonist Travis Bickle, played by Robert De Niro, crosses a subway platform. It's night and there's a crazy drummer parked under the lights, banging out solos.

The guy they used in the movie is a real person. His name is Gene Palma. If you lived in New York then, you've seen him on sidewalks and subway platforms with his sticks and his skins. He does styles. Chick Webb, Gene Krupa, Ginger Baker, all the while keeping up a running patter. People pass and toss quarters into his drum case, or the odd single or even a five.

That's me. I'm that drummer. I'm doing it for fun. I'm doing it because I have no Plan B. I'm doing it because I can't do anything else.

50. MARTY FOR DINNER

I work for two years on the new book. My seventy-seven-year-old agent Bart—fictional name Marty—is getting impatient. Again from *The Knowledge*:

> Marty phones me the Sunday after Thanksgiving. He wants to meet for dinner. He has big news, he says. He wants to know when I'm going to be finished with the book I'm working on now. "When will we have a draft I can take out to the town?"
>
> "Three weeks or a month. I just have to crack the ending."
>
> Marty has already told me the big news, about a week ago, but he has forgotten that conversation. The word is that a hot young editor, Christopher Brand (the son of Everett Brand, who edited Faulkner) wants to read my new manuscript. Christopher had wanted to publish an earlier book, my second one, titled *Bethesda Transfer*, but he couldn't sell it to his bosses at Random House. Well, says Marty, now Chris is at Houghton Mifflin in Boston with his own imprint; he's looking for a young writer whose first work he can bring out. "But you gotta get it to me fast," Marty says. "Half a dozen other agents are trying to get their clients in to Chris too. We have to beat 'em! There can only be one Hot New Writer."

SIDEBAR: TINSELTOWN FLASH-FORWARD

SIX YEARS LATER I'M again in North Carolina. I'm forty-three years old now, working on a movie called *King Kong Lives*, one of the all-time lamest motion pictures—whatever you do, do not see it—written by me and my writing partner, whom I'll call "Stanley" for reasons of privacy.

North Carolina is a right-to-work state. No unions. Dino De Laurentiis is producing the film here, along with a couple of others. He has built his own zero-frills studio (no soundproofing in the soundstages) near Wilmington.

Casting for *King Kong Lives* has still not been completed. Linda Hamilton has signed to play the female lead but finding the male star is proving to be problematic.

Dino is shooting another movie beside *King Kong Lives* at his North Carolina studio. It's called *No Mercy*. The stars are Richard Gere and Kim Basinger, with the Dutch actor Jeroen Krabbé superb as the villain. *No Mercy* is actually a pretty good movie. If it comes on cable, give it a squint. They're shooting it on the stages and out in the swamps around Wilmington.

The best thing about Dino's studio is it has a great chow hall. Whoever set the place up has found some local Carolina ladies who know how to put together a true Southern feed. Plus Dino has brought in a giant copper-plated cappuccino machine. Nobody on any of the crews misses a meal at Dino's commissary.

One lunchtime I'm entering with Stanley. I'm on a rant about how hard can it be to find a decent male lead for *King Kong Lives*? "The guy doesn't have to be super-handsome. He just has to give off respectable male vibes." I point across the commissary to a line of crew members with their trays, waiting to get fed—carpenters, electricians, prop masters. "Look at those guys over there. Twenty normal American working men. We could throw a dart and find a leading man."

There! I point to the third crew member in line.

"What about that guy? See, in the blue shirt. What's wrong with him? Why can't we find somebody like him?"

I look again.

It's Richard Gere.

51. MY FIRST SCREENPLAY

How did I get into the movie business? Here's the short answer: my book bombs.

I get it in too late. It's my fault.

My agent Marty meets me at the Oyster Bar in Grand Central Terminal. We didn't get the manuscript in on time, he says. Christopher Brand has gone with another young writer.

My book is dead.

"I'm sorry, my boy. We were so close."

Marty tells me that of course he'll keep submitting the manuscript. But I can see in his eyes that the moment has passed. The publishing biz is notoriously incestuous. Every editor knows which books every other editor has passed on or elected not to acquire. No one dares take the career risk of bidding on material that others have already rejected.

Marty tells me he took the train to Boston himself, hand-delivered the manuscript to Christopher Brand's office at Houghton Mifflin. Chris was heartbroken as well. But it was too late. Chris had signed the contract with the other writer.

"I feel so inadequate," Marty says in his Old World cadence. "I have let you down. You placed your faith in me and I have proved unworthy."

I feel ten times worse than Marty. Not for myself but for him.

"It's my fault, Marty. I'm the one who let you down by getting the book to you so late. I can't believe you took the train to Boston. No agent in the world would do that. Only you. I apologize to you, Marty. I failed you."

There's a term in the movie business—though I didn't know this at the time—called the All Is Lost Moment.

This is mine.

I'm thirty-seven years old. This is my third novel. I have poured my heart into it. It's as good as I can do, and it's dead, dead, dead.

I don't have it in me to spend three more years writing number four.

For four days I'm seriously teetering. My cat has stopped going outside. He's looking at me funny. Clearly he's thinking, *How am I gonna clean up the mess after Steve blows his brains out? Or get him down from the hook when he hangs himself?*

Then at the fifth midnight I have a flash.

Why don't I try writing screenplays?

I'll move to LA. Why not? I've failed as a novelist. Why not go out there and fail as a screenwriter?

My friend Jennifer has worked as an assistant to a Hollywood agent. I phone her at one in the morning.

"You have to write a sample," she says. "A screenplay on spec. No agent's gonna take you on without something they can show around."

Next morning I'm standing in the dark outside Barnes & Noble waiting for the doors to open.

I buy a $3.95 paperback, *How to Write a Screenplay*.

52. MY FIRST SCREENPLAY, PART TWO

I have consumed way too much Hemingway and Kerouac and Henry Miller during my years on the road, and I have interpreted them all wrong. Somehow I have internalized the following ethic of twentieth-century authordom:

Everything you write must be true. It has to have actually happened—and have happened to you. Otherwise, you are cheating. You are a fake.

Every character has to be based on a real person.

You yourself (or a thinly veiled version of yourself) must be the protagonist.

You are not entitled to write any scene for yourself or describe any action that you have not literally taken. Otherwise, you are lying, you are a charlatan, etc.

I'm sitting at my Smith-Corona, next to the noose I have planned to hang myself with, staring at the chapter in *How to Write a Screenplay* titled "Character Development." I come to a decision.

I will never write another word about myself.

No characters based on me. Ever. No issues founded on my own shit.

Instantly a massive weight falls from my shoulders. I hate myself anyway. What a relief to jettison this subject forever.

From now on, I will never write a character based on anyone I actually know or any person who exists in real life.

From now on, I will make everything up.

53. MY FIRST SCREENPLAY, PART THREE

I write a prison story.

I have never been to prison.

I know nothing about prison.

To my astonishment, the pages fly. Scenes crackle with energy. I start making up wilder stuff. In the Main Library at Forty-Second and Fifth, I'm checking out books on penitentiary construction. I'm throwing in physical details I know nothing about. What does a cellblock look like? Is it possible to escape through the sewage system?

More to the point, I'm making up characters. Characters who are neither me nor anyone I've ever known.

It's working.

Friends who read the script actually like it. They think it's true. Several tug me aside conspiratorially.

"Steve, where did you do time?"

Book Five

STANLEY DUPLASS

My van, my cat, and I arrive in Hollywood during the heyday of the "spec script," meaning a screenplay written without a deal or contract, entirely on speculation.

Movies have replaced music and TV—not to mention novels and nonfiction—as the dominant popular medium. Studios are desperate for material. Valets at Morton's, clerks at Blockbuster, hippie waitresses at The Source are making deals for three hundred grand, eight hundred, a million.

I am so happy to have given up the dream of writing a novel.

This is the movies!

It's La La Land!

Anything is possible.

Screenwriting, I realize, is the ultimate entrepreneurial endeavor for the penniless. You don't need a camera. You don't need a cast. You don't need a budget. All you have to have are a typewriter and 120 sheets of paper.

Write at the beach. Write in your car. Write in the kitchen of your apartment in Silver Lake or Echo Park. Don't have a degree from USC? Nobody cares. English is your fourth language? No one gives a shit.

Even if you can only type with two fingers, you can bang out three acts in twelve-point Courier, single-sided, on three-hole punch (cover optional) with copper brads to bind the mess together. Nobody can stop you. You can write *Star Wars*. You can write *Chinatown*. You can write *Apocalypse Now*.

The following is my output over the first half decade in the shadow of the Hollywood sign. Each screenplay takes about six months to write.

Crazy Davis
Gold Bug
Spaced Out
Under the Sea
"X"
Sergeant Sweetheart
Eagle Feather
Jimmie Shelter
Inspired
Jackknife
Born to Shop

Have I sold any? Please.

I have found work, though. I have a job as a copywriter at a business-to-business ad agency across from Bullock's Wilshire just north of Koreatown. I have a tiny apartment in Brentwood. It has a back stairway so Mo can get out and roam the neighborhood. He's happy. I have hope again. My dream is to sell the van and make payments on a Toyota Starlet.

No, I am not getting laid.

No, I am not a regular at parties in the Hollywood Hills.

How do I keep going?

One, I have a good agent. His name is Mike Werner. He runs a one-man boutique agency in Westwood. His other clients have written *Alien, The China Syndrome, Blue Thunder*, many others. Mike is the real deal. To be with him means something.

Two, I'm learning. Each failed project teaches me something. Mike mentors me. He gives me good screenplays to read. He introduces me to his other clients. He gets my stuff out to the town. Some of it gets me meetings with real producers. It hurts, what they say about my heroes or my climactic scenes or the unshootableness of 90 percent of the material I'm writing.

But I'm learning.

This gives me hope.

55. FACT AND FICTION

Before, when I tried to write the truth, everything came out false. Only now, when I've given up on facts, am I starting to write the truth.

Truth is not the truth.

Fiction is the truth.

This is a monumental breakthrough for me. But there's this about breakthroughs. They only last five minutes.

My prison script goes nowhere. Neither do the two sci-fi screenplays that follow, or the detective story, or the family trucking saga, or the army story, or the one about the sculptor in San Francisco or blah blah etc. any of the next dozen I bang out on spec.

56. WHY AM I DOING THIS SHIT?

Why am I living like this? Am I crazy? I'm forty-two years old. I just got the third paying gig of my life—a five-hundred-dollar rewrite on a porn flick.

I should be ashamed of myself. I should be shopping at Safeway in sackcloth and ashes.

Yet—can I tell the truth?—I'm happy.

I'm a writer. I've tried everything else. Nothing works. I can't write ads, I can't drive trucks, I can't dangle from superstructures a hundred and twenty feet above the Gulf of Mexico.

I'm a writer.

This is what I do. It's the only thing that makes me happy, or at least keeps me from slitting my wrists.

I have this. This page in front of me. This white space. This story in my head. That's all I've got and you know what? It's enough.

It's enough.

57. KEEP WORKING

I'm working on a low-budget action script for the director Ernie Pintoff. I drive each morning to Ernie's house in Outpost Canyon. We work side by side at the big oak table in his front room. The following is from *Nobody Wants to Read Your Sh*t* (2016).

> Ernie never spoke to me about anything except the movie we were writing. I wasn't sure he even knew my name. But little by little we started getting to know each other. One day during a break he asked me what else I was doing when I wasn't working for him. I told him I had written three novels that never got published—and I was constantly hammering out spec screenplays that also didn't sell.
>
> "Keep working," he said.
>
> I could tell this was a piece of serious wisdom from a veteran who had been through the wars, but I wasn't really sure what Ernie meant.
>
> The next day I asked him if he wouldn't mind elaborating. Again he said, "Just keep working."
>
> Then Ernie's fiftieth birthday came around. His wife Caroline threw a big party. When the event was over, Ernie and I wound up in the kitchen together, washing the dishes. Ernie had recently been diagnosed with cancer. He had had cancer twice before and survived.
>
> "Keep working," he said. "Don't turn anything down. Porn flicks, slasher movies, free stuff for friends.

Don't get precious. You're young, you're learning. Keep working."

He cited three reasons:

"One, working means you're getting paid. I know you're getting peanuts for this job. It doesn't matter. It's money, it's validation. Every buck means you're a working pro, you're toiling in your chosen field.

"Two, when you work, you learn. Everybody has something to teach you. A grip will show you something about lighting, an editor will drop some pearl about what to keep and what to cut. Even actors know something.

"Three, you're making friends. Some kid who's schlepping coffee today may be a producer tomorrow. He may buy one of your specs. An actress you do some free work for today may get you hired for a rewrite six months from now."

There's a sad ending to this story. Ernie died a few years later. Our little action movie never got made.

But I took a lot of jobs because of what Ernie told me, and I never regretted any of them. He gave me the best advice I've ever gotten.

"Keep working."

58. TEAMING UP

One day my agent Mike takes me out for coffee. Mike believes in me, but he's getting tired of taking my scripts out and coming back with nothing.

"What would you say to me teaming you up with another writer? An older, established writer. You'll be the junior partner. You'll work your ass off, but you'll be working. You'll be making money."

The older writer is Stanley Duplass. That's what I'm calling him, to respect his real-life privacy. He's one of Mike's clients. I've met him in the office. Stanley is a colorful show-biz character, known all over town for his eccentricities. He also happens to be a genius. He's had two hundred-million-dollar hits, including one with his name above the title.

I think about it for .02 seconds.

"How soon can I start?"

59. "I'LL BE OVER AT NINE-THIRTY"

Stanley and I shake hands. "Let's work at your place," he says. "I'll be over tomorrow at nine-thirty."

My place is a Spanish-style bungalow off Robertson south of Pico. Stanley shows up at 12:30

Next day: 1:30.

Day after: 2:45.

This goes on for a month. I'm pleading. "Stanley, I'm sitting here doing nothing! What's the problem? Why can't you get here on time?"

But six weeks into our partnership, Stanley is still arriving mid-afternoon. We work for a desultory hour, then find ourselves so exhausted and dispirited we have to quit.

Finally, one morning I say to myself, "Steve, just start. Don't wait for Stan."

When Stanley arrives that day at one-thirty, I have seven pages to show him. We go over the work. Stan has a bunch of smart things to say. We tweak the pages, make plans for the next day's work, then Stan goes home.

The next day I have six more pages. We do more good work.

It dawns on me that that this is what Stanley has wanted all along. He is not really a writer-writer. He's a producer-writer. He needs a partner who is a writer-writer.

Stanley gets us work. In meetings, he does all the talking. Stanley is more than a little nutty, but studios and production entities are hot to work with him. He has delivered two huge hits. He is a brand.

Working with Stanley, for the first time in my life I am making enough money to pay the rent.

60. STANLEY AND ME AT THE CINEPLEX

Over the next five years Stanley and I—or I on my own—complete the following screenplays.

King Kong Lives
Above the Law
Hard to Kill
Million-Dollar Mystery a.k.a. *Kiss Me and Pull the Trigger*
Prime Directive
Total Recall
Born Bad
Free-Jack
Cryptic
The Nighttime Guy
Zero Odds

Some of these get made. Most don't. Of the ones that do become movies, I pretty much hate all of them. From *The War of Art (2002)*:

> The first professional writing job I ever had, after seventeen years of trying, was on a movie called *King Kong Lives*. I and my partner-at-the-time [Stanley Duplass], hammered out the screenplay for Dino De Laurentiis. We loved it; we were sure we had a hit. Even after we 'd seen the finished film, we were certain it was a smash. We invited everyone we knew to the premiere, even rented out the joint next door for a post-triumph

blowout. Get there early, we warned our friends, the place'll be mobbed.

Nobody showed. There was only one guy in line beside our guests and he was muttering something about spare change. In the theater, our friends endured the movie in mute stupefaction. When the lights came up, they fled like cockroaches into the night.

Next day came the review in *Daily Variety*:

"... Stanley Duplass and Steven Pressfield; we hope these are not their real names, for their parents' sake."

When the first week's grosses came in, the flick barely registered. Still I clung to hope. Maybe it's only tanking in urban areas, maybe it's playing better in the burbs. I motored to an Edge City multiplex. A youth manned the popcorn booth. "How's *King Kong Lives*?" I asked. He flashed thumbs-down. "Miss it, man. It sucks."

And yet...

And yet you're working. You're getting paid. Stuff that came entirely out of your head is actually being filmed. Actors are speaking your lines. Who am I to complain? I'm sleeping in a bed. I'm not bagging Winesaps at five-thirty in the morning or dangling off a cable crane a hundred and twenty feet above the Gulf of Mexico. My house has heat. I've got a refrigerator. I can afford a cheeseburger.

Best of all, I'm learning. Getting your ass kicked working in the movies is the greatest education a writer could want. Most of the learning happens off-screen. Shit that never gets made. Stories you write for love and can't sell to anybody. That's okay. That's how it always has been and no doubt how it should be.

The myth is the City of Angels is brutal. In fact it's kind. It's forgiving. You don't need mainstream gigs to survive. You can make a living in the spaces in between.

Not every script has to be produced or even optioned to buoy you with positive energy. Sometimes you come close. A bona fide star or a serious working producer will fall in love with something you wrote. Or his or her partner or development VP will become a champion for it and for you. There'll be buzz. People will get excited.

You get excited too. Even if a deal goes nowhere, or there's no deal at all, you feel like you're in the arena. You're making noise. People are learning your name.

The next one!

The next one will break through!

I'm in a rented tux striding with my hi-glam date into a premiere. Flash bulbs are popping; the paparazzi are straining from behind the velvet rope. I spy a photographer up ahead on the right, turning his lens toward me. Suddenly his buddy catches his arm.

"Don't shoot! He's nobody!"

62. AGAINST ALL ODDS

A meeting at Twentieth-Century Fox runs late. I come out in the dark. The Fox lot is huge; alleys between soundstages seem to lead nowhere. I grope around for half an hour, getting more and more lost. Finally I spot my van, in a lot surrounded by a chain-link fence. The gate is locked. I can't get in.

I decide to climb.

The fence is really high. I get to the top and am just throwing my leg over when I chance to look down. There, beneath the security floodlights, in a back-alley space behind production offices, sit two roll-off dumpsters, each one the size of a truck trailer. Both are open at the top. I can see down into them.

Both are filled to the rim with discarded screenplays.

From *The War of Art:*

> I had been in Tinseltown five years, had finished nine
> screenplays on spec, none of which had sold. [This is
> before teaming with Stanley.] Finally I got a meeting
> with a big producer. He kept taking phone calls, even
> as I pitched my stuff. He had one of those headset
> things, so he didn't even have to pick up a receiver.
> The calls came in and he took them.
>
> Finally one came that was personal. "Would you
> mind?" He indicated the door. "I need some privacy
> on this one."
>
> I exited. The door closed behind me. Ten minutes
> passed. I was standing out by the secretaries. Twenty
> more minutes. The producer's door opened; he came
> out pulling on his jacket. "Oh, I'm so sorry!"
>
> He had forgotten all about me.

64. THINGS YOU LEARN IN TINSELTOWN #1

I'm writing a low-budget action flick with a director whose bread and butter is episodic TV. I show him a scene where the hero asks another character a question.

"No," says the director. "The hero never asks a question."

65. "I DON'T LOOK GOOD IN THE DESERT."

I'm working with Steven Seagal on an idea about Area 51. The premise—Steve's idea—is that ETs are real and that he—a version of his *Above the Law* character—becomes involved with a real extraterrestrial and helps him escape. I'm spitballing a scene out loud for Steve. In the scene his character dashes across an open stretch of desert to a secret building where the ETs are being held.

"Stop!" says Steve. "The scene doesn't work."

"Why not?"

"I don't look good in the desert."

For six seconds I'm speechless. That's the dumbest reason I've ever heard to kill a scene.

Then I think about it.

Steve is right.

He doesn't look good in the desert.

66. "I DON'T ASK QUESTIONS. I ANSWER THEM."

Back to the low-budget action flick. The director cites Jack Lord, the star of *Hawaii Five-O,* with whom he has worked many times.

"Jack Lord always says, 'I don't ask questions. I answer them.'"

I'm thinking, *That is the most egomaniacal statement I've ever heard.*

But the more I think about it, the more I get Jack Lord's meaning.

Jack Lord is saying that the hero powers the narrative. The hero must have an intention. He must be relentless in his passion to achieve that intention.

Indeed a detective must interrogate suspects, and to do so he must ask questions. But these interrogatives cannot be baffled, weak queries. They must be focused, aggressive actions.

Jack Lord is right about heroes.

"I don't ask questions. I answer them."

A year later I pitch Steven Seagal a project I'm convinced is perfect for him. Do you remember a TV series called *Mr. Lucky*? The setting is a luxury yacht, the *Fortuna*, that operates as a floating casino outside the three-mile limit. Gamblers zip out and back aboard lushly-appointed launches. The TV series starred John Vivyan as Mr. Lucky, with Ross Martin as his sidekick, Andamo.

The series was based on a movie of the same title starring Cary Grant and Laraine Day.

Key points about the character of Mr. Lucky:

One, he always wears a tuxedo. He's dashing, urbane, sophisticated, but with a mysterious past, like the Humphrey Bogart character in *Casablanca*. Each week a new drama unfolds aboard the *Fortuna* as fresh characters come out from shore to gamble or to pursue their desperate destinies.

Two, the character of Mr. Lucky is central to every episode. He solves every mystery. He kills every bad guy. Every female guest falls in love with him. It's his yacht. He's the star. Everything in every story revolves around him.

Three, he never asks questions. He answers them.

Why do I pitch this idea specifically to Steve?

Because he looks great in a tuxedo.

I'm with Stanley at the Nuart on Pico. It's two in the afternoon; we're watching *Out of the Past* (1947), starring Robert Mitchum, Jane Greer, and Kirk Douglas.

Before I started working with Stanley, I had never heard of *Out of the Past*. I had never heard of film noir. Now I've fallen in love with both.

Stanley is opening my eyes to the canon.

Stanley never schools me overtly. He doesn't say, "You must watch *Battleship Potemkin*." Or "What? You haven't seen *The Sand Pebbles*?" He just cites them in making a point about some scene or story we're working on.

Now I've gotta see 'em.

Stanley loves noir detective stories. Under his tutelage I inhale *The Maltese Falcon, The Glass Key, Farewell My Lovely, Double Indemnity, Kiss Me Deadly, The Big Sleep,* not to mention *Gun Crazy, Touch of Evil, Pickup on South Street* and in French with subtitles *Elevator to the Gallows, Bob le Flambeur,* and *Le Samourai.* I'm glued to Bogey in *High Sierra* and Cagney in *White Heat*, riveted to Edmond O'Brien in *DOA* and Charles McGraw and Marie Windsor in *The Narrow Margin*. When Tristar remakes the latter with Gene Hackman and Anne Archer in 1990, Stanley is beside himself. "That shoulda been us! We should've made it!"

From Stanley I'm learning the concept of acquiring properties. You don't have to come up with every idea out of your own steaming skull. You can find stuff. Forgotten classics. B-movies gathering dust. Many are owned by estates of deceased authors. The families will practically pay you to take the rights.

Stanley is geeked out for science fiction. He mines the catalogs of Philip K. Dick and Robert Heinlein, Frank Herbert, Ursula Le Guin and a hundred other writers no one but out-and-out freaks and fanboys have heard of. Once a week he comes in with a pulp short story from *Analog* or *Fantasy*. I ask, "Is it any good?" Stanley's answer is always the same. "It's a mess."

Stanley is glad the story's a mess. He's seeking a bold idea, an innovative what-if. "Sci-fi short-story writers can't finish a concept. There's never an act 3 and usually not even an act 2. But some of these stories have brilliant premises."

This, I'm learning, is how films get adapted. You find something that's got pizzazz but that doesn't work. You make it work. Then you sell it.

"Studios and financiers," Stanley explains, "need a reason to back a new project. Pure spec scares them. No executive wants to risk his job standing up for something totally new. But if you can come to them with an Isaac Asimov story or an article by Arthur C. Clarke, you make it easier for them to say yes."

For me, this is a PhD week after week. Stanley and I are taking fascinating but unfulfilled material and trying to make it work. It's happening all over town. *Do Androids Dream of Electric Sheep?* becomes *Blade Runner*. *We Can Remember It for You Wholesale* is made for the screen (by Stanley) as *Total Recall*.

What is science fiction? It's a technological spin on a philosophical or metaphysical problem. What if a memory could be erased? What if a person could travel through time? What if you and I could live forever?

69. GENRE AND GENRE CONVENTIONS

Stanley and I want to write a contemporary film noir. Can it be done? Lawrence Kasdan pulled it off with *Body Heat*. Can we do it too?

Step one for Stanley: What existing property can we steal, option, or copy?

We cue up *Gun Crazy, Body and Soul,* and *They Made Me a Criminal*. Unearthing these relics is an enterprise unto itself. We search the shelves of Vidiots on Pico, the Blockbuster at Olympic and La Cienega. We scour the archives at the Academy. We find *Nobody Lives Forever, Brute Force, I Walk Alone, Kiss the Blood Off My Hands*. We watch *Key Largo, In a Lonely Place, Brother Orchid, Vice Squad, Dark City, Bad For Each Other, Too Late for Tears.*

Many of these, Stanley knows already. In the seat next to me, I feel him squirming with delight. It's contagious. I fall in love with these creep shows too.

We're studying something else as we watch these B&W classics.

We're studying conventions.

What scenes, what story beats does every film noir have? Why does Lauren Bacall always play the same role? Lizabeth Scott? Edward G. Robinson? Why does the hero always get beaten up, often multiple times?

We study modern detective stories. *Harper, Klute, The Long Goodbye*. The filmmakers are doing exactly what we're doing. They're mining the conventions and obligatory scenes of a prior era's classics and retooling them for contemporary audiences.

When I worked in advertising in New York, I was always amazed (and morally outraged) when veteran, award-winning art directors, seeking to work up a new ad, would go straight to the magazine files and steal any layout or graphic concept they could find. "What do you think Leonardo did?" one salty AD asked me, when I objected to his larceny.

He quoted Olivier.

> Mediocre artists borrow. Great artists steal and make better.

"It ain't stealing, kid, if you put a spin on it."

71. DELILAH

As Stanley and I are seeking inspiration among the archives, I decide to do a little property acquisition of my own. One of the books my friend Paul Rink loved (and inspired me to fall in love with) is *Delilah* by Marcus Goodrich.

Delilah is a war story. The title is the name of a Navy destroyer—a coal-fired, flat-deck four-piper from the WWI era. Marcus Goodrich himself was one of the founders of the Writers Guild—called the Screenwriters Guild in the early 40s. He was married to Olivia de Havilland. An interesting dude, now ninety-two and in a care facility. His works are under a conservatorship managed by his attorney.

I option *Delilah* for twenty-five hundred dollars.

Wow.

I'm a producer now, or at least starting to think like one.

What do writers hate worse than death? Someone who acquires their material and changes it without their permission.

Such an act is malign. It's dastardly. What rotten SOB would do such a thing?

All of a sudden, it's me.

Without a word to Mr. Goodrich, I begin tearing his superlative novel, published in 1941, to shreds. *Delilah* is set on the eve of WWI. I change it to WWII. One of the central characters is an Irish monk. I make him Japanese. I change the theme. I reconfigure the characters. I turn the climax inside-out.

The worst part is it's fun. I hate myself for appropriating (or misappropriating) material from a writer I revere. But the book has had fifty-five years to make it to film and it hasn't happened yet. Maybe I can help it.

I write *Delilah* without Stanley. I don't even tell him I'm doing it. I've got other ideas too.

72. "STEVE, YOUR EGO IS GETTING OUT OF HAND."

Four years into our partnership, I begin agitating with Stanley for more credit. He won't give it to me. I understand his position. His credibility as a producer depends on the quality of the spec material he delivers. His position vis-à-vis any acquiring entity is, "If you want this great script, you have to give me credit as a producer."

Stanley has a manager. His name is Tony Ridio. One day Tony phones. "Steve, we need to talk."

Tony's livelihood depends in large measure upon Stanley's success. I understand this too.

Tony and I meet at Brent's Deli on Ventura Boulevard in Encino.

"Steve," Tony begins, "you're a good guy and I like you, but your ego is getting out of hand. I want to talk to you before you wind up doing something you'll regret."

The waitress comes with Tony's Reuben and my pastrami on rye. Around the deli, booths are populated by other Hollywood one-on-one confabs just like ours. Tony waits till the waitress has set down our plates and departed.

Tony says he knows I'm frustrated. He can see that I believe I'm doing all the work and getting none of the credit. He understands this, he says. He doesn't fault me for feeling that way.

Tony cites three or four screenwriting teams I'm familiar with—two-person teams that are getting work and getting movies made. One I'll call Mike and Jim. In fact, Mike is sitting at another booth in Brent's Deli right now, by himself, going over some notes.

"Steve, everybody in town knows Mike does all the work in that team. Jim doesn't even live here. He's in Madison, Wisconsin, for Christ's sake. He doesn't get into town two times a year!"

But, Tony says, Jim has the name. Jim has had hits on his own. Jim is the star. Mike does the writing, but Jim brings in the jobs.

Tony is telling me that if I keep agitating with Stanley for more credit, I'll kill the golden goose. He urges me to open my eyes and take a realistic view of my position.

"Steve, you could have the script for *Gone with the Wind* under your arm, written by you alone. You could take it to every studio in town. You know what would happen?"

I know.

"But if you took that same script into those same studios, written by Stanley and you, you'd be cashing a check for seven figures.

"Stanley is the brand," Tony continues. "He's had hits. Stanley's name gets you the meetings. His reputation gets you the work.

"Stanley has had two partners before you, Steve, and he's had hits with both of them. Do you know what that means in this town? It means Stanley is perceived as the key element. He's the variable that consistently produces success."

Tony can see he's getting through to me. My pastrami on rye is sitting untouched.

"Steve, I understand your frustration, and you're right to feel frustrated. You *are* busting your ass and you *are* doing terrific work. But Stanley has had hits with partners before you and he'll have hits with partners after you. The bottom line is this:

"If you want real credit, you have to sell a script on your own and have a hit on your own."

Stanley and I have worn a groove in the freeway between Venice and DEG, the De Laurentiis Entertainment Group offices on Wilshire Boulevard in Beverly Hills.

We always take my van because Stanley's eight-year-old Tercel is packed to the windowline with screenplays, treatments, outlines, contracts, litigation documents, along with his collection of woolen mufflers (for warmth), orthopedic shoes, Coast Guard watch caps, surgical trusses, knee bindings, shoe orthotics, and cases of vitamins and dietary supplements. Stanley is a gale-force hypochondriac. He enters any room carrying an eighteen-by-twenty-four cardboard box that contains the two tennis balls he braces against his sciatic nerve when he sits, his vials of essential oils, his Intestinal Mover capsules, and his TENS pain machine, which he immediately plugs into the nearest socket while affixing its electric pads to his ear lobes or whatever limb or extremity is plaguing him this day. Stanley is excruciatingly attuned to the exterior or interior environment. If the cabin temperature of any vehicle varies as little as one degree Fahrenheit from Stanley's ideal, he insists that said vehicle be pulled over and adjustments made.

I have no trouble accommodating Stanley. Like I said, he's a genius.

When I first team with Stanley, he has one mega-budget sci-fi project in the works for producer Dino De Laurentiis. This is incredibly good news for me because it means a paycheck from day one.

Stanley and I do rewrite after rewrite on this picture. When one is done, Dino wants another.

In meetings at Dino's office, it's Stanley, Dino, me, and a stenographer, almost always a chain-smoking, Cote d'Azur-shades-wearing femme of mystery named Silvia, who speaks Italian, Portuguese, Spanish, French, German and English. Silvia and I never open our mouths. Wait, I take that back. Silvia bursts occasionally into scolding harangues in Italian aimed at Dino, to which he responds at first with irascible impatience before caving in and, with a great flurry of hands, dismisses Silvia and returns to Stanley.

Dino himself is a bona fide legend of cinema. He came out of the postwar Italian film renaissance as a producer of unwatchable trash along with immortal neorealist classics like *Bitter Rice, La Strada*, and *Nights of Cabiria*. His peers are Federico Fellini, Vittorio De Sica, Carlo Ponti (Sophia Loren's husband), Michelangelo Antonioni, and Roberto Rossellini.

Dino himself was married to Silvana Mangano, whom he discovered as Miss Rome and made into an international singing star and screen siren. By the time of his death in 2010, Dino will have made more than five hundred films (including *Serpico, Three Days of the Condor, Blue Velvet*, and the Jeff Bridges-Jessica Lange remake of *King Kong*), thirty-eight of which were nominated for Oscars. At the same time, he is an incorrigible schlockmeister. When Dino starts a sentence with, "Wait! I have idea!" Stanley's nervous system goes into nuclear seizure.

What I love about Stanley is he lives to do great work. Though he has made millions, he gives almost all of it away, to family, to friends, to Hollywood freeloaders. All Stanley cares about is making great movies—and getting credit for them. As I said, he's a producer.

Dino is also a producer, but from a whole different universe. Dino's desk in carved mahogany arrived from Florence, legend has it, in a packing crate with the names of two Popes on the sides. Dino presides from behind its august mass like the Dapper Don in bespoke suits shipped by air freight from his personal tailor in Milan. As a filmmaker he has no shame. Will a movie sell? Will it put asses in seats? Dino's for it. He can turn an immortal script into dogshit and he will if left to his devices.

There's no way not to love the guy.

I love Italians. I love postwar Italian cinema. I could watch *Rome, Open City* over and over, as well as *The Bicycle Thief, Paisa, Fear, Stromboli*, not to mention *La Strada, La Dolce Vita, Two Women* and *The Damned.*

Dino was part of this. He made his bones digging up scripts and raising a few thousand lira to mount the sonsofbitches. God bless him. He doesn't stand above five foot seven, but he is a giant.

Across the desk from Dino sits Stanley with his pain machine and his sciatic tennis balls. Stanley himself, as I said, has made a fortune, but he gives away every dime to ne'er-do-well relatives, friends, and moochers. His place on the Venice canals is a hive. Open his fridge. All he's got is Calistoga water and sheep yogurt. Dandruff flakes fleck the surface of his winter-in-Wyoming muffler. But he stands toe to toe with Dino. Stanley is looking to history. He sees his own place in cinema and, truth to tell, he's got one and it's up there.

Dino, to his credit, recognizes this and respects it. He shovels offbeat projects at Stanley. "You write this for me?"

"How soon?"

"Two weeks."

Stanley glances to me. I nod.

"I got another," says Dino.

We sign up for that too.

The struggle between Dino and Stanley is like a closed-cage death match between Cesare Borgia and Leonardo da Vinci. The *condottiero* is looking for sensation. He'd put tits on the Virgin if it'd sell. But Stanley/Leonardo lives for the ages. He seeks, if not deathless art, then some story or scene that will live forever.

Dino, addressing Stanley, indicates me. "How come he never speak?"

"Who?"

"Your friend. Um ... uh—"

"Steve," I offer.

"He speaks," says Stanley.

"I like him. He's good boy. You let him speak."

This is my life for the next four years.

How do you learn to write? This is how. You toil as a galley slave under the lash.

Row us from Venetia to Alexandria.

You do.

You want to.

You learn by being left alone, like me on the road in South Carolina with the fried electric plug in the rainstorm. Life forces you to solve a problem, and when you've solved it and gotten it wrong, you are sent back to get it right.

Collaboration works too. You sit in rooms with your partner or your boss, beating your brains out trying to make a story work. I come up with ten ideas. Stanley rejects nine. And he's right. He has picked the one good one. Each time I ask myself, *What did I learn? Why did he pick that one? What is he seeing that I'm not?*

And how can I teach myself to find that?

Then there are times when Stanley is wrong. You learn even more from these. You learn that you can be right without the master's approval.

74. VOODOO LOVE

I'm developing a crush on Silvia, the stenographer/woman of mystery from Dino's office. This is unexpected. Silvia is married. She smokes horrible Romanian cigarettes named Marasestis; her breath reeks of Iron Curtain contraband. Plus she's 100 percent not my type. Her nail polish is black. I'm almost certain she belongs to a coven. She drives some kind of Stalinesque military staff car with no discernible insignia and no license plates.

Still, I'm a goner. I drive her home one night after a late meeting at Dino's. We wind up making out in my front seat, between Silvia's lung-busting inhales of Moldavian tobacco, parked outside the house in Beachwood Canyon where she lives with her husband.

This is not me. I don't do this. But I can't stop myself. In story meetings with Dino, I find myself stealing glances at Silvia over her steno pad. I'm devastated if she doesn't glance back.

I have a producer friend named Ilana who also works for Dino. From her I learn that Silvia is having a transatlantic affair with an Italian screenwriter—a great one, Ilana says—who may or may not be the father of her daughter. Then there's Dino's private pilot, also Italian. Silvia is banging him too. "Oh," Ilana adds as I'm leaving. She herself has made out passionately with Silvia behind the coffee machine in the movie-poster locker.

Silvia is a mesmerizing talker. Her cross-cultural Euro-know-how passes from gypsy legends and sixth-century *maleficia* to necromancy, thaumaturgy, and virgin sacrifice. She's Jewish. She schools me in the Kabballah. I'm suddenly swimming in Gnostic lore and tales of dybbuks. I learn the Aramaic roots of the *yetzer hara*. Diagrams of the Tree of Life litter my back seat.

Silvia introduces me to the *Kybalion*. She lends me her solitary copy, on pain of death to return it. This, Silvia tells me, is the fountainhead, the source of all wisdom, from the greatest occult avatar of all—Hermes Trismegistos, Hermes Thrice-Great, of ancient Egypt, he whose wisdom founded Masonic thought and powered the alchemists.

"You and I," Silvia tells me while extracting my hand from beneath her skirt, "possess no material reality. We are nothing but thoughts in the mind of the All, as Pip and Magwitch and Mister Micawber were thoughts in the mind of Dickens."

I gotta say, I love this shit.

Meanwhile my friend Tony has come from California to stay with me. Tony, you recall, is my role model for self-discipline. He has become a hands-on healer. He has come to Los Angeles to study with Rosalyn Bruyere at the Healing Light Center in Glendale. I'm not making this up. Rosalyn has powers. She is being studied at UCLA. The CIA has had her out to Langley.

Pretty soon I'm commuting to Glendale myself. Tony has been taught how to do past life regressions. He practices on me.

It works.

75. WHERE DO IDEAS COME FROM?

Tony gives me a book, *The Nature of Personal Reality* by Jane Roberts. Have you read this? It's a channeled book, i.e., Ms. Roberts didn't "write" it; instead, she deliberately put herself into an altered state and "received" the book page-by-page from an "entity" whom she calls Seth.

Seth speaks through Jane. Jane goes into a trance and this stuff comes out. Where does Seth live? Among the stars. In another dimension. Jane doesn't know and Seth doesn't tell her. The cool part is that if Seth is dictating and his words break off at Minute 127:23 (because Jane has some real-world emergency and has to leave town for three weeks), Seth's dictation picks up again three weeks later at the exact spot where he left off.

The Big Takeaway is the idea that

We create our own reality.

Wait a minute. This is what Silvia's *Kybalion* says. It's what the Kabballah declares. It's what I'm experiencing with Tony in past life regressions.

Meanwhile I've started reading *A Course in Miracles*. The thrust of this tome is that nothing we see or feel is real. We're inventing it all, based on our conditioned assumptions.

When you're a screenwriter, you're constantly looking for ideas. The search never ends for a "What if?" that might generate a story.

In science fiction, the "what if" is usually technological. Time travel. Transplanted memories. But some what ifs are psychological or metaphysical. What if there really is a devil? What if there are previous lives?

What if all perception is illusion?

What if we *do* create our own reality?

A movie is starting to come to me.

What if it's true that we create our own reality, that the world as we experience it is manufactured moment to moment by our own thoughts? Could I write a story about this? What genre would it work best in?

A cop story!

What if we had a burnt-out NYPD homicide detective? He's seen nothing but the dark side of human nature for years. The world of evil has become his reality. Could he somehow, via his own mind—even against his will or without his conscious awareness—create some super-dark reality that then took on a life of its own?

Short version: I write the script.

It comes out great.

How do I know it's great? Because when I show it to Stanley, his immediate instinct (after putting his name on the title page) is to protect it from being ruined. "We can't show this to Dino! He'll destroy it in ten seconds with his terrible ideas."

Stanley comes up with a title.

Cryptic.

I love it.

He begins brainstorming a campaign to get the script out. "We can't just give it to CAA [Stanley's agency]. They'll flood it to all the obvious targets. It'll get read by assistants who won't get it. It'll be dead in a week."

We have to go directly to filmmakers and financiers. Stanley compiles a list. Who's gonna respond to the material? Who's free to make it? Whose name can bring in financing?

Stanley loves young directors, foreign directors, directors fresh out of advertising or video. Why? Because they're hungry. They've got talent but they haven't yet been spoiled. Actors love about-to-be-discovered directors as well. A hot new director can attract a big-name star. And these young directors are affordable. Financing becomes possible via unconventional channels. We don't have to sell out to a big studio that will crush us.

Stanley's name opens the door to such hot young helmers.

We take *Cryptic* to the director of a recent sleeper hit.

We get it to the newest young guy out of Cannes.

Through Stanley's manager Tony we reach the latest sizzling ad guy.

All three love it.

All three want to do it.

I haven't said a word to Silvia though I'm seeing her, now, three or four nights a week. I don't want to jinx anything. In my quiet moments, which are damn few, I reinforce myself.

You did it, Steve. This one is fucking good. And you did it virtually alone.

I ask myself what this means. Am I getting better? Have I learned under Stanley's tutelage?

Or is the secret that I'm free of Stanley? Is *Cryptic* as good as it is because I could write it on my own, trusting my own instincts, without tailoring it to his tastes or what we imagine his name will help sell?

It's November. Silvia has to leave for Italy for a month. She says it's on business for Dino, and I'm sure it is, but she'll also almost certainly be with her screenwriter boyfriend. Do I really care? I'm so guilty for seeing her behind her husband's back that it's almost a relief to see her off.

Stanley finds financing for *Cryptic.*

He puts together a package of foreign pre-sales. With this in hand, he can approach US studios and production companies or go to the film-financing division of an actual bank. Stanley finds one in Belgium and another in England. Can we shoot interiors at Elstree or miniatures at Pinewood? The New York stuff can be shot on location in a week, two tops, to save money.

Right now the script has both our names on it.

That makes sense. We have to do that to sell it. It's the whole basis of Stanley's motivation. It enables him to take producer credit and to demand that his name be above the title.

I'm flattered. It's validation big-time.

By now I've told Silvia. She's in Ravenna, writing me via Telex.

"You can't do this," she says. "This is your movie. It must be your name on it!"

Silvia's right. It's time for me to move out of Stanley's shadow. I hint with him a few times. I'm not trying to usurp anything. Of course, Stanley will be the producer. He's putting together the deal! What will he care if I get sole screenplay credit? He can have shared story credit. Shit, I'll give him full story credit.

At this stage, the assignment of credits is strictly up to the writers. Later the Writers Guild will step in to adjudicate. But now it's between Stanley and me.

I want the title credits to read

Screenplay by
Steven Pressfield

Story by
Steven Pressfield and Stanley Duplass

I call Stanley up. I'm in the kitchen of my little house off Robertson, standing by the toaster waiting for a blueberry Pop-Tart to come up. I can hear Stanley snorting on the other end.

I make my pitch.

"If that's the way you feel, " Stanley says, "I can no longer work with you."

And he hangs up.

My pastry pops, seared to a cinder.

Stanley means it. He'll blow up the whole picture before sacrificing credit.

Our partnership is over.

Stanley has dumped me.

BOOK SIX

DINO

77. YOU CREATE YOUR OWN REALITY

My life is flashing before my eyes.

How will I get work?

Stanley's the brand. He's the name. No one is going to hire me all by myself.

I once counted the All Is Lost moments in my life. I came up with twelve. Another time I did it and the total was forty-seven.

But this now with Stanley, this is the Big One.

I'm fifty-one years old.

The sell-by date for a screenwriter is probably thirty-one.

Stanley can get work at an advanced age because he's had hits. He's a player. Me? I'm nobody. I'm fucked.

78. I SPEAK

I place a call to Dino.

Silvia's still in Italy so I go through the chain of assistants. Finally Dino's voice comes on the line.

"You have called to speak?"

"I have. Can I come in?"

Dino's office is being remodeled, so we meet, he and I, beneath the chrome cappuccino machine in the top-floor dining room overlooking Wilshire. Dino has heard about the *Cryptic* debacle between me and Stanley.

"Why you don't bring this script to me?"

Dino knows the answer. He minds, I can see. But he understands. And he has certainly discerned the power dynamics between me and Stanley.

One of Dino's non-Silvia assistants brings cappuccinos in porcelain Lavazza cups with demi-tasse spoons and a micro bowl of lump-turbinado sugar.

At home I have rallied to a new hyper-disciplined regimen.

I've got enough in the bank to last a year. A screenplay takes me six months to write, That means I can bang out two before going broke.

That's what I'll do.

I'll reach out to every producer/studio exec/development person I know and tell them I'm on my own and I'm available.

If I can find work or sell one of the two scripts, I'll stay in LA.

If not, it'll be Plan Z.

I start each day with the gym at five, then home for a power breakfast like my liver-and-eggs special from *Bethesda Transfer* days. I'm at the keyboard by seven, going nonstop to noon. I must make each lunch pay in the sphere of getting myself out and into "the town." Rest and social stuff, reading and meditation take me to day's end. Lights out at eight and on to the next day.

My two script ideas: a multiple-personality thriller with a female lead and an action-heavy contemporary film noir set in the California desert. Why these? Because they're castable, affordable, saleable to TV and foreign. I will never get a studio film made; I don't have the name.

And both ideas are fun. I like them. I can do some cool shit with them.

"Come with me," says Dino. He takes his cappuccino and rises. This is the first time I have ever been alone with Dino and the first time, other than our brief phone call, that he has ever addressed a word to me outside of a meeting headed by Stanley.

Dino leads down one hall and into another. We enter a storage room. One-sheet movie posters lie flat in an open, floor-to-ceiling steel cabinet. I'm thinking, *Is this the room where Ilana made out with Silvia?* The posters are in Italian, French, and Spanish. A row of filing cabinets squats against another wall.

"You speak Italian?"

I shake my head. Dino slides a drawer open, takes out a movie script, and passes it to me.

LA CITTA' ETERNA

The piece is in Italian, with the writer's name—a male I don't recognize—beneath it.

"I want you translate."

It's common knowledge that Dino never reads scripts in English. He has people who translate everything, even letters and memos, into his native tongue.

"I don't understand," I say. "You've already got this in Italian."

Dino dismisses this.

"I want in English. Ten grand cash. I need in three days. You do?"

I'd love to. "But how can I translate it if I don't read Italian?"

Dino glances to the doorway. I turn. Silvia stands there.

I'm thrilled to see her. "I thought you were in Italy!"

She says nothing, only smiles.

"You work with Silvia," Dino says. "She tell you what script say, you write in English."

"When would you like me to start?"

"Tonight."

One thing about Dino: He pays. I do the job in thirty-six hours. The check arrives twenty minutes later by messenger.

Meanwhile the first of my two scripts—the contempo film noir—is going gangbusters. Am I deluding myself or have I actually become a decent writer? I don't dare show pages to anyone (bad karma) but my cat and I are psyched by what's coming out.

At the same time I'm nosing around a bit, just out of curiosity, on the bio of the screenwriter of Dino's script.

Oh, I forgot to say. I love the script! It's the best screenplay I've ever read. Better than *Chinatown*, better than *The Godfather*. Who *is* this writer? The name on the title page says

Carlo Quattronomine

That can't be a real name. Who *really* wrote this? Antonioni? Rossellini? Fellini himself?

The story is set in Rome in the Open City era immediately after WWII. Its hero is a handsome but half-assed detective who gets involved in investigating the murder of the scion of one of Italy's richest and most venerable families. The Bad Guys are the post-war American carpetbaggers, the Russians, various mafia bonebreakers and one gorgeous but deadly heiress of the rich Italian family.

I love the script so much I approach Dino. Can I buy it?

Dino laughs.

"This script will win Oscar three years from now."

He wants it for himself, he says. That's why he had me translate it.

Meanwhile I've seriously fallen in love with Silvia. Before, it was just a crush. Now I'm over the cliff. I still haven't slept with her, or even spent a moment with her outside of working on the script. "We must be careful," Silvia insists. "My husband. I cannot break his heart."

Until one post-midnight. "Can you come over? Carlo is here."

Carlo the screenwriter?

"Are you serious? The guy who wrote *La Citta Eterna*?"

I jump in my van and speed over.

Silvia waits outside in the shadows. We can't go in. Her husband is there. He has had a confrontation with Carlo. In fact Carlo has fled. Silvia kisses me. She's drunk.

"Dino wants to sell you the script."

"What? He told me himself he loves it. He says it'll win an Oscar three years from now."

"You don't have to buy it for cash. Just put your name on it."

"What are you talking about? I can't do that."

"Why not?"

"Because I didn't write it."

"You translated it."

"You and I translated it. And all we did was copy what was already there. And besides, why does Dino want my name on it? Does he even own the script?"

Silvia won't answer.

"He doesn't, does he? Carlo owns it."

Silvia turns away.

"Carlo won't sell it to Dino. Will he?"

I'm beginning to get it. A power struggle is happening over the script.

"What's going on, Silvia? Why is this so important to you? Where is Carlo? Why can't I meet him?"

"Because he is in trouble! That story in the script... it's true! The murderers, they are real!"

"Who is Carlo? Is he Fellini? Is he Antonioni?"

"He is Carlo!"

"Tell me the truth!"

Silvia repeats her explanation, then replays it, then tells it again. Each time it's different. I can't tell if Carlo is trying to force Dino to buy the script or if Dino is trying to compel Carlo to sell it. Maybe Silvia's telling the truth about the script being based on an actual crime. Could Carlo really be in danger from forces who don't want their dirty deeds exposed?

I don't know. All I know is I can't participate.

"Will you put your name on the script or not?" Silvia demands.

"I can't."

"Then I can't see you no more."

She stubs out her stogey in my dashboard ashtray and pushes the passenger door open. The last I see of her are the heels of her Via Veneto boots as she stomps up the walk to her house, enters, and slams the door behind her.

Like Stanley, Silvia has dumped me.

I'm getting calls on *Cryptic*.

I still haven't shown it to Frank, my new agent. (My original agent and dear friend Mike has tragically died; a heart attack at age fifty-two.) Stanley won't let me. He's with CAA. Every deal on our stuff together must go through Creative Artists Agency.

"What the fuck?" Frank bawls into the phone. "I'm getting offers and I don't even know what the damn thing's about! I look like an idiot."

I tell Frank not to worry. Stanley will never let *Cryptic* go forward anyway. I can hear Frank groaning on the other end.

"And what's this Italian script? You can't keep me in the dark like this!"

"What script? What are you talking about?"

"It's here in front of me. *Eternal City* by Steven Pressfield."

"That's not my script."

"It better be. It's getting raves all over town."

I finish both specs—the film noir and the identity thriller—by month ten. What are the odds against selling even one? Hundred to one? Higher?

But amazingly there is heat.

An indie producer almost finds financing for the first one, *Joshua Tree*. The deal falls through at the last minute. But one of his assistants is the fiancée of an Israeli producer with a ten-million-dollar production fund. She takes the script to him, seeking a producer credit herself. He passes. Four other almost-deals fall out. I'm in meetings and doing free rewrites on other producers' projects.

Suddenly the Israeli possibility comes back to life. But I have to cut my price in half, then in half again.

The deal comes together. My new agent Frank attaches an actor from his stable. That actor brings in his wife as co-lead. Tax considerations fall into place. If I'll sign for low, low dollars and agree to two free production rewrites, it's a go.

I'm stoked.

It's a movie!

Without Stanley.

My first ever on my own.

It takes me a second to recognize my new agent's voice.

"Frank?"

"I need you in town tonight."

I'm on location in Lone Pine in the Eastern Sierra, shooting *Joshua Tree*.

"Tonight? It's already four-thirty and I'm five hours away."

"I've got two offers on *Eternal City*. One's a six-month option for $250K. The other's an outright buy for a mill."

"What does that have to do with me?"

"It's your movie. You're the writer."

Frank brings me up to speed. Sources unknown, for reasons unknown—perhaps Dino's company, perhaps some other entity—have flooded the town with the script. It's everywhere, my agent says, and it's generating heat everywhere. Frank confesses that he has had the script copied two dozen times and messengered to potential buyers or "elements," i.e., individual directors, producers, actors. My name, Frank tells me, is on the title page.

"But I didn't write it, Frank. It's by Carlo—"

"I just hung up from the Writers Guild. They're holding the regis-tration copy. It's in your name. You're the writer."

I tell Frank I can't come back. "I know you're hot to make a deal. I'd love to make one too. But how can we? No matter what crazy shit is going on, the script isn't mine."

Here I must interject an insight to the writer's mind-set.

At the same time this call is happening, I'm working furiously on *Delilah*, the Navy story I optioned from the novel by Marcus Goodrich.

The truth? My head is so deeply into *Delilah,* I'm barely even registering this other stuff. The motel I'm staying at in Lone Pine has a "Cary Grant suite," in honor of the George Stevens' classic *Gunga Din*, which was shot here in 1939.

I've got it.

It's my room.

I've rearranged the furniture to match my little house behind the big house. I've got my same table and my same Smith-Corona. I am feverishly into *Delilah*.

I've finished two screenplays this year. *Delilah* will be the third.

And it's good.

My year is up. Year and a half actually, as events have turned out. The first script, *Joshua Tree*, has been shot and released. It went straight to video. It's unwatchable. When I see it for the first time, my colon seizes up for three days.

The second picture, the psychological thriller, has been made too. I'm invited for a glimpse of the dailies. Exiting, I consider suicide. Only hope against hope keeps me going. That, and the fact that my adapted screenplay for *Delilah*—plus a newer original Western, *Under the Double Eagle*, that's even better—are making the rounds. Both are getting serious attention.

I attend the premiere of the psychological thriller. The movie is so bad I'm literally sinking into the carpet, attempting to become invisible. Forty minutes in, my heart feels the size of a cherry tomato. I tiptoe up the aisle, hiding my face in shame.

The movie's director is a friend, a well-regarded producer. I've done two projects for him with Stanley. This film, the thriller, is his first opportunity at directing. Because of the respect he commands as a producer the town has let him test his wings.

Exiting, I spot him. He's in the shadows of the SRO space behind the rearmost row of seats.

He is bent double, crouched over his knees, his head in his hands.

83. MY AGENT FRANK

I'm sitting across from Frank in his office.

Every agony I've endured since my marriage and my life first went down in flames has played like *Battleship Potemkin* across the cineplex screen of my mind for the past four days—since the calamitous premiere of the thriller on top of the straight-to-video catastrophe of the film noir.

Was it all for this?

Is this the payoff?

Can there be a single shittier writer than me in all of Hollywood?

Frank has phoned, insisting on an in-person meeting. Will he dump me too? Will my van make it to Buras, Louisiana?

Frank's office is in a high-rise in Century City. He keeps me waiting forty-five minutes. I'm getting up to bolt in despair when his secretary, Miriam, appears.

I follow her in. Frank crosses from behind his desk and throws a bear hug around me. He's six-foot-four and 230. I'm muttering into his neck, something about how unwatchable both my movies are, how sorry I am ...

"What?" Frank pulls back. "Are you crazy?"

He tells me he's just made an option deal for *Under the Double Eagle*. Twentieth-Century Fox has acquired the script for Troph Productions, Patrick Swayze's company, for Swayze to star in.

"But what about these other fiascoes?"

Frank stares at me.

"You have no idea, do you?"

"Of what?"

"Of how this business works."

Frank makes me sit. Miriam brings a Perrier for him and a coffee for me.

"Your movies suck, right? You're humiliated. You're heartbroken. Your career is over, right? Bullshit!"

Frank plants himself in the Eames chair across from me. He leans forward.

"Do you know how many writers have gotten *one* movie made in the past eighteen months, let alone *two*? Who cares if they've tanked! Who gives a shit if they went straight to video? Nobody's gonna see 'em anyway. All they see is a title in the trades with your name next to it. What are they thinking? They're thinking, whoever this new writer is, he wrote something that attracted actors, that brought in a director, that found financing, that got *fucking made!*"

Frank rises from his Eames chair. He's pacing.

"Has anyone in this town read any of your other scripts? Fuck no. But they've seen coverage. An assistant drops a ten rating on *Delilah*. A D-girl pops a rave for *Cryptic*. And I haven't even mentioned *Eternal City*. Stop! Don't tell me you didn't write it. I don't give a rat's ass and neither does Spielberg's development VP or the guy who reads for Marty Scorsese. All they hear is the thing is *fan-fucking-tastic* and your name's on the title page.

"You're a force, Steve. Based on scripts you've written, two deals have been made. Seven hundred and eighty-six people have been put to work. Movies have appeared. Real motion pictures shot on real film. Your stuff has juice, buddy! *You* have juice!"

Frank says he's fielding offers from three studios right now for the Italian script.

"But we can't sell it!" I declare.

"I don't *want* to sell it, my brother. It makes you twice as hot to have mystery. Let the town guess. The more times we turn 'em down, the higher your quote goes!"

"But I've bombed, Frank. Everything I've written has gone straight into the toilet."

"Who gives a shit? You're the hottest writer in town!"

Two more years pass. For the first time, I'm writing scripts that I'm actually proud of. I can't sell 'em, of course. And the ones I'm doing for hire or as optioned specs never actually make it to the screen. But, as I said before, and as Frank keeps reinforcing, a writer can make a decent living under the Hollywood sign even if nothing gets made and his name never appears in the credits of an actual released film.

This town.

I'm doing a free rewrite at MGM when a producer friend, a woman, spots me on the bungalow's front porch and plops down in the chair beside me. She asks what I'm working on besides this freebie. I hesitate.

"That can't happen," she says.

"What do you mean?"

"You not being ready when someone asks that question. Look around," she says, indicating the soundstages and the production offices that stretch in every direction for hundreds of yards. "Every studio has a slate. Fox, Disney, Warners... they've all got a lineup of pictures they're making and more in the pipeline. Every producer on this lot has a slate, and every producer and actor and director on every other lot has a slate. I have a slate. You have to have one too."

My friend makes me tell her every script I'm working on right now, whether it's under option, looking to get picked up, or still in the typewriter.

Under the Double Eagle
Delilah
Montana

Ismaila
Cryptic
Mister X
Canvas
Line of Scrimmage

"That's a slate," says my friend. "You and I and everyone else hustling in this town has got to have a slate. We're a business, just like SONY and Paramount and MGM, and we're competing with SONY and Paramount and MGM."

I'm proud of these screenplays. Every one is different, every one has an original concept, and every one is by me alone.

Under the Double Eagle with Patrick Swayze comes close at Fox, but "goes into turnaround."

I fail bringing *Mister X* to a level worthy of production.

Same on *Montana,* a contemporary remake of *The Searchers.*

I'm a business.

I'm competing with other businesses.

Delilah is hot for a few weeks, fades, then rekindles only to swoon again.

Canvas is a fictional version of Georgia O'Keeffe's life in New Mexico in the twenties. I almost get it going twice. Then a film about another female artist tanks.

Line of Scrimmage gets optioned by Disney before a new CEO comes in and kills all existing projects.

I'm a studio.

I've got a slate.

For about six weeks, Stanley (on his own) reignites *Cryptic*. He finds a director. A distributor signs on. Stanley is inches from securing financing when the director can't wait any longer; he takes another film.

Then one day the strangest thing happens.

I get an idea.

In truth, I'm *seized by* an idea.

I *have to* do it. I have no choice. There's only one problem...

The idea is not for a movie. It's for a book.

86. MY AGENT FRANK, PART TWO

One thing I love about Frank is he actually cares about the material he represents. He gets excited over a good idea. He sweats out casting and choice of director. He's in there. He's fighting.

He likes it that I'm a spec writer. It's fun for him to have me come in and pitch ideas. He'll carve out a couple of hours (unheard of in this town) close the office door and listen with total attention while I try out four or five specs on him.

"I love the second one but we can't do it. Tri-Star is in production on a project just like it."

That's how Frank will save me half a year of effort.

If I pitch a genre that I love, say a Western or a film noir, he'll cite the box office stats for the past five years. "Forget a Western, even a contemporary. No studio will touch one after [and he'll list half a dozen bombs I've never heard of.]"

The good news is when Frank loves an idea, he's in it with both feet. He is there in the birthing stall. He has slapped the baby's butt.

Now here I am, sitting across from my partner, my buddy, my soul brother in the crystalline sunlight of Frank's nineteenth-floor Century City office.

"I've got good news," I say. "And I've got bad news. Then I've got worse news."

Frank wants the good news first.

"I have an idea for a story. I'm seized by it. I can't not do it."

"What's the bad news?"

"It's not a movie. It's a book."

A groan escapes Frank's breast. "What the worse news?"

"The book is about golf."

Frank actually loves golf. He's a good golfer. He belongs to Hillcrest. I've played with him and his dad a bunch of times. But now he's thinking of golf as *the subject of a story*.

A second, deeper groan ascends.

"A book," he says, with the same tone and inflection he might employ to pronounce the word *turd*.

Frank regards me balefully. "A book about *golf.*"

"I know, I know..." I start to defend the idea.

"Steve," my agent says, "let me explain something that you may not fully appreciate. You have a career now. You're in demand. A big part of that is because of me. It's not just the phone calls and the submissions of material. It's not the schmoozing at parties and the ten thousand ways I get your name in front of people. It's my own reputation. It's my taste in writers and material."

"I understand, Frank, believe me..."

"Wait, let me finish. Do you know what you writing a book means? It means a year minimum away from the industry. Away from meetings, away from lunches, away from every form of contact. This town forgets people in a week. A month and you're ancient history. Twelve months? Every ounce of work I've done—and you've done—over five years goes down the tubes.

"Look," Frank says, "I understand you're seized by this idea. I get it. I respect it. It shows you're a real writer. But you can't do this. You can't do it to yourself, and you can't do it to me."

My heart is sinking. Everything Frank says is true. He *has* busted his ass for me. A year away *will* put me in the category of extinction. And I'm thinking something else. A novel about golf? Could there possibly be a lamer idea? I'll spend a year or more and the thing will sink without a trace.

"I'll make you a deal, Steve." Frank shifts in his seat. He had been addressing me from behind his desk. Now he rises and comes around. He perches on the edge of the Eames chair, inclining toward me.

"Write the golf thing. I can see you love it. It's clear you've gotta do it. But do it on your own time. Weekends, nights, whatever your off-hours look like. Meanwhile keep writing movies. Keep bringing me material, keep going to meetings. Maintain a presence in the town. Keep taking assignments, and when you get 'em, give them your full attention and your best, truest effort. That's fair, right?"

Frank is studying my face. I'm hopeless at hiding what's inside me.

There's no way I can keep writing movies, at least not for now. I've got to do this book full-tilt and full-time..

"Who's gonna represent this opus?" Frank says. "I'm not a literary agent. I can't take the book to publishers, even if I wanted to, which I don't, not to mention you haven't even written the motherfucker. You haven't, have you?"

"I haven't started."

"Well, don't!"

Frank asks me who I imagine will be the audience for this book. Is there a market for novels about golf, for Christ's sake?

A great void opens in my belly. I've been in meetings like this. At the end of each tenure in advertising, my boss, whoever he or she was (and they were always friends and always good people) would sit me down seriously and sanely, like Frank is doing now, and ask me what I hoped to accomplish by leaving a good steady job to try, yet again, to write fiction.

They were right of course. Just like Frank is right now. He's even more right because I owe him. I'm not just throwing away *my* future.

"You're gonna do this, aren't you?"

"I don't know, Frank. I can't argue with anything you say. You've been great to me and I'm in your debt..."

"But you're gonna do it."

We part over a handshake. Frank doesn't see me to the door. Outside, his assistant Miriam shoots me a look I've never seen before.

Something makes me turn back.

Frank's door is already closed. I knock and poke my head in.

"Frank," I say. "Did you just fire me?"

BOOK SEVEN

STERLING LORD

Reading these pages over, I feel I've left something out that I really wanted to convey. It's about beauty. It's about my love for this country.

I spent nine weeks in Israel a few years ago researching *The Lion's Gate*, a nonfiction book about the Six Day War of 1967. One testament I heard over and over from the men and women I interviewed was how much passion they felt for the land of Israel. I don't mean its politics or religion. The land itself. Combat nurses and fighter pilots told me over and over, often with a catch in their throats, how much of their youth had been spent trekking and exploring, always on foot, the hills and plains of the Holy Land.

That's how I feel about America.

One thing about being a trucker and living the trucking life is you see the dawn every morning. You're on the road when the sun comes up. The high, wide windshield is like a 3-D IMAX screen exploding, if not always with straight-up beauty, then for sure with the horizon-to-horizon energy and horsepower of the United States.

I'm with Woody Guthrie. I'm with Walt Whitman. Count me alongside Jack Kerouac, Ken Kesey and Gary Snyder. I love this fucking place.

I know it sucks. I see the shit. I read the hatred and the suspicion and the crazy waste of time that is most of our lives. I see the drunks and the wife-beaters and the dirty cops and the criminals at the top of the food chain. I feel the blood that has soaked into the earth from men and women beaten with barbed wire and hung from trees while children looked on and cheered. None of that is lost on me.

But this country is still beautiful. I know that hasn't come across in these pages as much I wish it had. That's my failing.

I'm thinking of a moment, I don't even know where or when, somewhere in South Carolina, I think, or maybe it was Georgia, when I pulled the truck over, late one summer afternoon, for a Grape Nehi and a Moon Pie at a country store. I parked the truck in the red-clay lot and stood beside the cab just as the sun was descending over a five-mile vista of tidal grassland and savanna. The Low Country. You can't describe that beauty without including the fecund stink of the marshland close enough that you can flick your Marlboro into it, or the burn of the sun on your face and the heat of your own back from six straight hours pressed against the rear of a corrugated cloth seat. I'm leaving out the diesel smell from the engine and fuel cook-off of the saddle tanks and the searing-hot vibrations of the steel block of the Cummins engine as it cools, not to mention the hiss and drip of the various oils and coolants and lubricating fluids. On my deathbed I'll forget people I loved and who loved me. Gone from memory will be entire years and even decades that were critical, live-or-die to me. But I'll remember forever that Moon Pie and that vista over the savanna.

One day, Mo doesn't come home. This is in LA, in my first apartment neighborhood off San Vicente—my grid of lanes and alleys with lots of speeding cars and drivers preoccupied with their careers and their social lives.

A few years later, I wrote the following in *The Knowledge*. It's about my time in New York City with Mo. "Teaspoon," as I said before, is my fictional name for him:

> I respect Teaspoon because he is his own man. I have no idea where he goes at night. I see him sometimes from the [rear window of my apartment, which has a staircase that leads down to the yard behind my building], padding across the faux vine arbor above the Portuguese restaurant's patio. I can hear him fighting with other cats in the alley behind the Chinese takeout. He roams as far afield as Nicolette's basement apartment, which is six city blocks away. I have no idea how he gets there. He navigates by cat radar and has since the first time Nicolette pet-sat for him. He shows up at her window and scratches till she lets him in. Nicolette is constantly insisting that I make Teaspoon an indoor cat ("He's crossing Eighth Avenue, for God's sake!") but I will never do that. My cat accepts the risks of city life and so do I.

I scour the neighborhood for two days. I put up signs with Mo's photo on every lamp post and power pole. I know if he's breathing, he'll make his way home. He has an ID collar with my phone number, so if anyone finds him…

On the third day I find his leg. Not the rest of him, just his leg. It's in a gutter between two parked cars. I sit in my van that night for hours, blaming myself. I could have found him sooner. I must've looked in the wrong places. Could the rest of him still be out there somewhere?

I decide that night to sell the van—or give it away if anyone will take it. I don't want to drive it any more without my best and truest friend.

Two nights later I get a call from Paul Rink's son Tony. Paul has had a heart attack. He's dead. The family buried him yesterday.

My mom dies twenty-seven days after that. I won't tell that story. It's even worse.

Six months have passed since that day in my agent Frank's office. I'm wrapping up the seventh and final draft of *The Legend of Bagger Vance*. The work has gone fast and good.

I may be crazy but I think I've got something.

I have no agent for the book. Frank is still furious at me for taking the time off to write it. He has stopped returning my calls.

I call my lawyer, Larry Rose. Does he know any book agents in New York?

Three days later Larry rings me back. His friend Jody Hotchkiss works as a books-to-movies agent for Sterling Lord of Sterling Lord Literistic, a prominent New York agency. I trade a couple of emails with Jody, get his address, and ship off the manuscript in a mailing box.

A week later Jody calls. Sterling has read the manuscript. He loves it. "We can sell this," he says. "In fact, I think Sterling's got a buyer already. Will you authorize us to be your representatives?"

Jody has another question. "How old are you?"

I tell him fifty-two. "Why do you ask?"

"From the book, I thought you'd be older." He pauses for a beat. "That's a compliment, by the way."

Three weeks later we have a publishing contract with Larry Hughes at Wm. Morrow and a week after that a movie deal with Jake Eberts, who has won Best Picture Oscars for producing *Gandhi, Chariots of Fire, Driving Miss Daisy,* and *Dances with Wolves.*

Jake himself calls a few days after that. A friend of his has expressed interest in directing the picture and possibly even starring in it. The friend's name is Robert Redford.

"Would you have any objections," Jake asks, "if Bob signs on?"

89. THE REZ

I give the van to my friend David.

David's wife Sarah is Navajo. She lives with her mother, who speaks only the traditional language, on the reservation in Arizona. David and Sarah have three daughters—Bah ("Warrior"), Kara, and Jolene. David's best friend is Sarah's brother, Bahi, the male version of "warrior."

Bahi is also a film editor. He's in town working on a Ron Perlman film. David's here with him. He's a prop master on the movie. It takes a couple of weeks before they get a few free days to ferry the van to Arizona. "Thanks for the truck, man," Bahi says. "It'll be a big help in the winter, carrying firewood and moving the sheep."

I will fly to New York to meet Jody and Sterling and to officially sign the book contract with Larry Hughes at Wm. Morrow. Jake Eberts will be in town too, but not Robert Redford. He's finishing another film. I'll also get to meet Tom Guinzburg, who has been a hero of mine for years. Tom has run Viking Press since the fifties. He was one of the founders of the *Paris Review*. He's also a decorated Marine infantryman from Iwo Jima.

How did these book and movie deals come together so fast?

It turns out that Sterling, who is in his seventies, has lunch every Monday with several peers of the New York literary sphere. He's been doing this for thirty years. Among those friends are Larry Hughes and Tom Guinzburg.

Sterling asks them to read the book.

They do. They both back up his judgment.

Larry makes an offer.

A few days later Larry is on an airplane. His seatmate, by chance, is Jake Eberts. By the time the plane lands, Jake is reading the manuscript.

Jake, not counting other bonds of friendship, is partners in the Sundance Catalog with Robert Redford.

Easy, ain't it?

91. A CAREER

Over the phone, Sterling congratulates me. "You know the first question any agent asks a writer who's just sold a book?"

I don't.

"What's the next one?

"No pressure," says Sterling. "But the sooner you can tell me your idea, the sooner I can sell it."

Jody and his secretary handle the details of hotels and lunches and schedules. We talk on the phone setting up days and times. "How much do you know about Sterling?" Jody asks.

He tells me Sterling represented Jack Kerouac. "He made the original deal for *On the Road*."

"Wow. I had no idea."

"The offer from Viking was nine hundred dollars. Sterling got them up to a thousand."

93. EAST AND WEST

I've never flown out of LAX before and certainly not on a ticket paid for by somebody else. My publisher, Wm. Morrow, will be picking me up at JFK, or at least they'll send a car.

I'm not going back to stay. My home is Los Angeles now. I have no intention of leaving. I'm flying East, as I said, to meet the people who will be central to my new life, or what I hope will be that new life. I will not be seeing my family. My dad died almost twenty-five years ago, and my mom, as I said, passed on a couple of months ago. My brother Mike lives in northern California.

This will be a business trip.

The flight is on American, first class. I've never flown first class. The seat is wide and deep, real leather, a window seat one row aft of the bulkhead. It's six-ten in the morning, way too early to have a drink. But I order one anyway, a White Label on the rocks, and take it down in three gulps. For some reason I'm thinking of another, earlier trip to New York, a crossing in my van. I can't remember the year, except it was November, like today, only colder.

I was coming from San Francisco then. The only work I could find there was as a driving instructor. I lasted half a day. The job seemed to me the utter zeroing-out of every honorable association I had ever had with operating motor vehicles over the road. I had a girlfriend then, a good one—someone I could have and probably should have married. She was a schoolteacher. Summer was ending and she was going back to work. Life was getting serious with the fall.

I just gave up. I can't do this anymore. I can't live this life. This on-the-road life. Maybe Jack Kerouac could do it, maybe Neal Cassady could. I can't. I've given it everything I've got for what seems like my entire youth, and I'm no better at it now than I was when I started.

I give up.

I'll go home to New York. I'll drive a cab. I'll take any job I can find. I have no shame and no ambition other than to work my way back to the sea-bottom of the middle class. If I can eventually find work as a copywriter, I'll take it.

I give up.

I leave out of LA forty-eight hours before Thanksgiving, having driven down from San Francisco the day before. Nights are still hot in Southern California, with Santa Anas howling out of the desert, but out farther, in real America, serious winter is coming. My plan is to take the 10 through Blythe to Phoenix, then down through Tucson to Las Cruces, where nights will still be warm, and past El Paso/Juarez into West Texas. I-40 is a better driving road but I don't want to risk snow at Flagstaff. Even my spare is a slick, and I don't trust my van's engine near any temperature where ice can form.

The man in the first-class seat next to me indicates my empty glass. He taps two yellow pills into his palm from a plastic prescription bottle, takes one himself, and offers the other to me.

I thank him but decline.

The last thing that happened, yesterday afternoon while I was packing for this flight, was Jake Eberts phoned to fire me off the *Bagger Vance* movie. Jake has four Best Picture Oscars but he's still the sweetest, most honorable gentleman you can imagine. It's excruciating, I can tell, for him to make this call.

"Jake, please, don't give it a moment of worry. I thank you! This is the first time I've ever been fired off a picture where somebody actually phoned me and told me."

Jake is concerned about my feelings. "You understand the movie business, Steve. Once a director comes on board—"

"Jake, truly, I'm touched and grateful that you're phoning me. The last time I was canned, I had to read about it in the trades. And the time before that, I was replaced by a writer who was represented by my own agent—and he, my agent, didn't tell me."

I ask Jake if the writer replacing me is a good one. "The best." He names the man and rattles off his credits. They're impressive. "He and Bob have a rapport. They've been working together. And he loves the project."

The flight attendant leans across my seatmate's lap and takes my glass. "Time for another before we taxi?"

I think about it.

"Why not?"

I talk to myself when I drive. I surrender to long, soul-exploring conversations—monologues really—that seem profound when I'm having them yet I can't remember a damn thing when they're over.

The theme on that last journey in the van was how crossing the country west to east is different from crossing it east to west.

The Mojave Desert starts past Palm Springs. It's good monologue country. When you drive in a vehicle as ancient and neglected as mine, you're like Saint-Exupéry flying at night over the Andes. Both ears hold glued to the anomalies of the engine. I swear I can hear—and feel—every spark plug as it misfires and every valve and tappet as it clatters and pings.

For me, America starts in New York. That's where I'm from, or, more accurately, where I fled from. Driving east to west is escape. It's adventure. Hope is the emotion, striking out from the Old US to the New.

West to east is different. It's defeat. Surrender. It's crawling home with your tail between your legs.

If I'm honest, I never really had that east-to-west dream. It wasn't like I set out imagining I could live, like Jack Kerouac, some "free spirit" version of life on the road. That fantasy insinuated itself by osmosis. I embraced it because I could find no other justification for the running-away life I was living.

I can't live that life any more.

I just want to get home.

I just want my poor six cylinders to keep firing.

Now on the plane I'm experiencing a different version of that monologue.

My new agent, Sterling Lord, as Jody told me, made the original deal for Jack Kerouac for *On the Road*.

West to east now is weird-coincidence vindication.

It's karma. It's serendipity. It's a circle closing.

From my seat by the window, I look down on the Mojave. Or maybe it's some other desert. Where are we anyway? Over Kingman? Tacking northeast to pass over Flagstaff?

I remember pulling over in a frozen Flying J truck stop in Lordsburg, New Mexico on that last trip east, sleeping in the van under every blanket I had.

By noon the next day I was past El Paso, heading southeast toward Sierra Blanca. The day was cold and nasty, with a hard gale beating out of the north. When cattle trucks passed, little storms of straw blew from the perforations in their corrugated flanks. You could smell steer piss blowing off the trucks' decks. A hi-box trailer had overturned west of Van Horn; Texas troopers had thrown up a go-around. Flares sizzled on the blacktop. Traffic snaked slowly forward.

A young couple was standing with their thumbs out in the gale. They were shivering in denim jackets and mud-crusted Western boots. Their luggage was two paper bags. Cars and pickups crept past without stopping.

I came up alongside and rolled down the window. "Get in. Where you going?"

"Amarillo," the cowboy shouted over the wind. He tugged the

passenger door open and piled in with his lady. "Thanks, man! We just got married!"

The cowboy stuck out his hand. "Name's Tate but everybody calls me Tater. Fucked up, ain't it?" He introduced his bride, Holly.

I told him I'd call him Tate if he liked.

"Too late for that, brother!"

There's no real front seat in a '65 Chevy van. The passenger slot is little more than a jump seat. Between that and the driver's seat is the cowling of the engine. Tate took that, leaving the softer sit-down for his bride.

The van crept in the lineup past the overturned tractor-trailer. Tate was rubbing his hands directly under the heater. You could hear the wind whistling through the cracks in the floorboard. Outside, scraps of desiccated tumbleweed whipped across the surface of the highway. Tate remarked on how every state north of here and all up through Canada is nothing but bare prairie without a tree or a bush to break the force of the storm.

"You know what they say. 'Ain't nothing between Amarillo and the North Pole but a barbed wire fence.'"

Holly snuggled up against him. They were in love. Cold or discomfort meant nothing to them.

I drove Tate and Holly to Odessa, about a hundred and fifty miles. I had to turn off I-10 to I-20 toward Abilene and would've had to turn due north further onto I-27 to Lubbock and Abilene to take them to Amarillo. Except suddenly Tate realized they had forgotten something back in Van Horn. Writing this now, I can't remember what the item was. A photo album? Whatever it was, it was clear they were both stricken by the loss.

"I'll take you back."

"You can't do that, man. You're heading home!"

"I'm not gonna leave you by the side of the road with the sun going down."

I drove Tate and Holly three hours back to Van Horn. It was midnight by the time we had tracked down their lost item and recovered it. They had no money to stay anywhere. Everything they owned was in those two paper bags.

We slept by the side of the road. I gave them the inside of the van, with the mattress. I slept under the vehicle, with a folded-up poncho for a ground roll and a doubled-up sleeping bag over top.

The next morning, I drove them east to Big Spring. I-27 cuts north there toward Lubbock and Amarillo. Tate was heading there to his uncle's ranch. He and Holly would work the winter and save money for whatever they would do next. They had no idea what that would be.

"Come with us," Tate says.

I ask him what he means.

"Work the winter. Get you a stake for New York." Tate says he'll get me on with his uncle. "You'll roll outa there next Spring with three or four grand in your pocket."

"Doing what?"

"Being a cowboy."

Tate says he'll teach me to ride a horse. No problem, he swears. I'll be a born hand in six weeks.

For about twenty seconds I actually think about it.

A cowboy.

Will that round out my American odyssey?

I drop Tate and Holly off at the Terrible Herbst where I-20 intersects with I-27 North.

I fill the tank and grab a couple packs of Hostess Donettes and a quart of milk. The dipstick is half an inch down. I add a quart of Valvoline, on sale at fifty-nine cents, wipe my punch spout with a paper towel and stow it behind my typewriter beside my jack and four-way tire iron. When I pull back onto the interstate, I can see Tate and Holly on the northeast shoulder opposite the truck stop, still carrying their paper bags, standing with their thumbs out in the West Texas gale.

The plane doesn't pass over Amarillo. Its flight path takes it north of Oklahoma City. Still I'm looking down at that raw winter prairie.

How do I feel about Robert Redford having Jake fire me? I don't blame him. *Bagger* is his movie now. I'd fire myself too if I were him.

What's next then, since I won't have any position on the film?

Sterling Lord, when I meet him, will ask.

In truth, I do have an idea.

I'm a studio.

I have to have a slate.

The idea is a novel—historical fiction—about Thermopylae, the battle from 480 BC between the Three Hundred Spartans and Xerxes' million-man invading Persian army.

I decide not to pitch specifics or even mention them. If Sterling asks, I'll say only that it's a period piece and that I'm deeply into it already. I really don't care what Sterling, or anyone else for that matter, thinks.

I love the idea. I'm seized by it, obscure and uncommercial as it almost certainly is. I'm going to do it, no matter what. I'll communicate that to Sterling and Jody if they ask, but nothing more.

My screenwriting career? It's over. That's the lesson from Frank.

It's books or nothing from now on.

A patch of turbulence strikes east of Oklahoma City. For about twenty minutes the plane bucks and bobbles. At last, the seat belt sign extinguishes. Carts return to the aisle. We're in smooth air again.

What does it mean to me that *Bagger* got picked up for a book and a movie?

It's epochal.

I will never say it out loud. I'll never acknowledge this to anyone except my brother Mike, who will understand. This book, this movie, however well or not-well received... this means the world. If I never do anything more, I'm satisfied.

It's been worth it.

Everything has been worth it.

And I'm going to keep going.

This is just the start.

96. GOVT CHEESE

If I had to name a favorite assignment when I drove for Burton Lines, it would be delivering surplus food to churches in those little towns along the Carolina coast. Other trucking companies had contracts for the Piedmont and the mountains, but Burton Lines took the loads that were bound for the eastern part of the state.

If you've never visited those coastal Carolina towns, you should go. Not to Wrightsville. Don't go there. Don't go to Wilmington. Don't go to Topsail Beach or Figure Eight Island or any other place you might have heard of. Go to the towns that don't appear in Google searches or Airbnb ads.

The towns I'm talking about are out past all multi-lane highways. Roads are two-lane blacktop. The towns themselves are six or seven miles apart, population fifteen hundred, three thousand tops. No bypasses around them.

On these surplus food runs, you're driving at two or three in the morning. You have to slow down through each little town, not just against the possibility of a local trooper ruining your night but because the settlements themselves demand respect. You pass the limestone statue to the Confederate dead, always the first thing as you enter, west to east. You're under elms and live oaks now. It's cool. Dense, verdant foliage gives the night air a taste.

It's different, passing down these lanes in a truck as opposed to a car. You're high. You're looking down on the sign for the feed and grain store or the Piggly Wiggly. Your cab is dim, lit only by the glow of the instrument panel, but the space is alive and trembling with the growl of the diesel and your own downshifting as you slow.

What I love about these trips is the idea that you're doing somebody some good. You're putting food on people's tables. Some honorable soul, maybe a pastor or minister, possibly an activist or even a state official, came up with the idea. Or it could have been the dairy industry or industrialized agriculture trying to turn a buck from excess production. I don't know. But the program has a good heart. It helps people.

I love the places we make deliveries to. Belhaven and Swan Quarter on Pamlico Sound. Gum Neck, Aurora, Mattamuskeet. Pink Hill. Sunbury. Today some of these towns have gentrified, but not much. Then they were straight-up boondocks. Half the acreage, if not more, was being sharecropped. I never made a delivery to a surfaced lot. Churches. Always churches and always lots paved with sand and seashells. The prisoners who loaded the truck at the start of the trip were black, the ministers who oversaw delivery and distribution of the food were black, the recipients were black.

This morning's trip is to Hertford, population 1,350, on the Perquimans River off Albemarle Sound, not far from Kill Devil Hills, Kitty Hawk, where the Wright Brothers first flew. I've arrived an hour early, five a.m., and pulled in and parked. I'm snoozing in the sleeper berth when I'm awakened by a rap on the cab's flank.

It's the minister. I pull on my boots and climb down.

"Driver, would you back your vehicle in yonder please, under that oak? We'll offload for you. Thank you. You may wait over there on the steps. Smoke if you like."

If you're a writer, sometimes you feel like a ghost. It's not you who's really producing the work. You understand that. You're a vehicle, like a truck is a vehicle. You deliver a load. When you're done, the trailer is empty. You seal it up and drive away.

As a writer I feel sometimes like I have no ego at all. I don't even possess a physical presence. Bringing food to people, the transaction is between the farm or the dairy and the ultimate recipient. It's exactly like writing. You, the driver, are just the medium. No one knows your name and you don't know theirs. You deliver your cargo this Friday and maybe you'll be back again two Fridays from now. Or maybe you'll be somewhere else. Maybe another driver will deliver the next load.

That's writing. That's any form of art. You feel in service to something, but you're not sure what. You hope what you do helps your brothers and sisters, but you know it's not coming from you.

Are they grateful?

You're grateful, just to be part of it.

I back the truck under the oak like the minister asks me. I do smoke, over by the steps where he pointed me. Spanish moss drips from the trees like lace curtains. The smells are of the earth and of smoke and sweat and the fishy stink of the channel just a few yards out across the two-lane. My truck smells of diesel fuel and tire rubber. I myself stink from driving half the night. Cigarette smoke clings to my hair. I love it. I love all of it.

You might imagine the recipients of government surplus to be destitute. But this morning, the first to pull into the lot is a broad-shouldered six-footer, twenty years old I'm guessing, in a sleeveless T-shirt that shows off his muscular arms. He's driving a Mustang convertible with the top down, radio blasting, and his girlfriend in the seat beside him looking like the prettiest Pointer Sister. He backs straight up to the trailer, springs out and pops the trunk. He greets the minister with a handshake and an exchange of congeniality that I can't hear because I'm too far away. Clearly the young man has been making this exchange, in this place, with this pastor, for years.

He and his girl load cartons into the Mustang's trunk. Powdered milk, USDA cheese, dehydrated potatoes, cases of canned yams, pinto beans, sliced peaches. Edging closer, I note a student parking sticker on the chrome elbow of the bumper.

NORTH CAROLINA STATE

A sweatshirt over the passenger seat says

WOLFPACK FOOTBALL

The cases of surplus are not light. They're food-in-bulk. It takes muscle to handle them. The church has a sort of warehouse/storage shed under a trellis of wisteria. Some boxes are being offloaded by the minister's helpers and set aside there. Parishioners continue pulling in. Most arrive in pickups and farm trucks, though the occasional tractor and even horse-drawn wagon turns in as well. Although it's clear that some of the recipients are regulars and have their favorite items that the minister and his volunteers unload and set aside for them, it's also apparent that early birds will show up to get the choice stuff. The football player is one of these. He has a list, from his mom, I imagine, as if he were shopping at Piggly Wiggly.

People keep coming. Three brothers (or maybe one is a cousin) in faded Oshkosh overalls, the oldest no more than ten, pull a Radio Flyer wagon with one wheel down to the rim. Older couples appear, no few on foot. Some push shopping carts.

The football player's girlfriend has crossed to the church steps. She's thanking the minister. A few minutes later in the distribution cycle a lady of around sixty materializes from the shadow under the live oaks. She's got one milky eye, tight gray curls, and a rubber-tire two-wheel cart pulled by a mule that looks about the same age as its owner. The lady's lower teeth are black from dipping snuff. She's barefoot. I see one of the minister's assistants intercept her as she turns her mule and wagon off the blacktop and into the church lot. Apparently she is not a member of this congregation. The assistant is explaining something to her. The lady is reacting with weary disappointment.

The minister observes this. He excuses himself from his conversation with the college-age girl and crosses to the wagon woman. I'm too far away to hear, but it seems as if he's explaining to this lady, with compassion and even anguish, that every item of surplus food has been spoken for by a member of the congregation and that these folks are in true need. Any article he might consign to another, he seems to be saying, would come off the table of families in serious straits. Clearly the minister is in distress at having to turn away this needy stranger.

Out of the corner of my eye I sense a form approaching. From behind me steps the athlete. He's carrying a heavy case of cheese with two smaller cartons balanced on top—powdered milk and dried pinto beans.

I turn back toward the Mustang. The fellow's girlfriend (or maybe she's his wife) has crossed to the car as well. She's hefting a fourth case from the trunk. She brings it over and sets it on the plank bed of the mule wagon. Grape jelly.

Five minutes later the wagon is making the turn out of the church lot to roll under the oaks onto the blacktop. The lady with the tight gray curls walks beside and slightly behind the mule, barefoot as she came, tapping the beast's shoulder with a wooden switch to both steer and drive. Directly to the rear of the wagon, still with its top down but no longer with the radio blasting, advances the Mustang, in first gear, protecting the mule and the lady.

There's something satisfyingly final about an empty trailer. The wood floor, the hollow echoing sound, the ribbed aluminum flanks, the high-box overhead with its two fiberglass skylights. I sweep the trash out—cardboard shards sliced by box-cutters, stomped-out cigarette butts, a spill of black-eyed peas from a torn packet. The minister's wife lets me discard the debris in the church's incinerator, a rusty fifty-five-gallon drum with triangular-shaped flue-holes cut around the bottom.

"Thank you, driver. You can close up now."

The tall, paired doors at the rear of the trailer swing together on heavy outboard hinges. You close the left first and lock it in place with the flange of the right. Each door has two steel swing handles that set the upright locking columns, top and bottom. You slot the handles into cradles flat against the now-closed doors and lock them down with drop-hinges. No need to padlock or seal them. The trailer's empty. I'll deadhead back to the terminal or to whatever pick-up point Hugh Reaves sends me for the next load.

The minister hands me the receipt copy of the bill of lading, signed. I fold it and tuck it into the pocket of my logbook.

"Thank you, driver. Is there anything further I can do for you?"

"No, sir. Anything I can do for you?"

The pastor shakes my hand. My watch says nine fifteen. I've been here since five, unloading since a few minutes after six.

I call in to the terminal from a pay phone at a country store outside Edenton, off State Road 71. Hugh Reaves says he's got a load of paper going to the American Tobacco Company at Bermuda Hundred, Virginia. The trailer's loaded and in the yard now, ready to go. He asks if I've got enough hours to make the trip.

I tell him I only used three last night. I can be back in less than that.

"All right, son," Hugh Reaves says. "Come on home."

I'm not a camera person. Nor was I particularly focused on chronicling anything during the period covered in the book. These few pix, alas, are all I've got.

New York, sometime in the 80's

Lesley + me
when the van was new.

My house in the country.
Photo by Cath Wright.

The redheaded cat.
photo by
Deborah Thompson Chromey

Photo by Tony Keppelman.

I'm second
from the right
in the back row

SARSAPARILLA MEDIA
(sass·per·illa)

My dad's favorite drink was sarsaparilla. He'd come home from work, look at my brother and me and say, "How about a glass of sass?" Naming this new company Sarsaparilla Media is a way of paying homage to my dad.

Printed in Great Britain
by Amazon

29162970R00169